Interior Design
Visual Presentation

Interior Design
Visual Presentation

A GUIDE
TO GRAPHICS, MODELS,
AND PRESENTATION TECHNIQUES

MAUREEN MITTON
IIDA, IDEC, CID

JOHN WILEY & SONS, INC.
New York • Chichester • Weinheim • Brisbane • Singapore • Toronto

Copyright © 1999 by John Wiley & Sons, Inc. All rights reserved.

Published simultaneously in Canada.

This publication is designed to provide accurate and authoritative
information in regard to the subject matter covered. It is sold with
the understanding that the publisher is not engaged in rendering
professional services. If professional advice or other expert assistance is required, the services of a competent professional person
should be sought.

Interior design and layout: Timothy O'Keeffe

Library of Congress Cataloging-in-Publication Data:
Mitton, Maureen.
    Interior design visual presentation: a guide to graphics,
    models & presentation techniques / Maureen Mitton
        p.   cm.
    Includes bibliographical references and index.
    ISBN 0-471-29259-1 (pbk. : alk. paper)
    1. interior decoration rendering. 2. Interior decoration--
Design. 3. Graphic Arts. I. Title
    NK2113.5.M58 1999
    729'.028--DC21   98-29271

Printed in the United States of America.
10 9 8 7 6 5 4 3 2 1

FOR
ROGER PARENTEAU

Contents

Acknowledgments ix

Introduction xi

Chapter One: ORTHOGRAPHIC DRAWINGS
    1 Introduction to Drawing
    2 Materials, Tools, and Equipment
    7 Understanding Orthographic Projection Drawings
    9 Orthographic Projection Drawings for Interior Environments

Chapter Two: THE DESIGN PROCESS AND RELATED GRAPHICS
    22 Introduction to the Design Process
    23 Programming
    28 Schematic Design
    40 Design Development

Chapter Three: PARALINE AND PERSPECTIVE DRAWINGS
    43 Introduction to Three-Dimensional Views
    44 Paraline Drawings
    48 Perspective Drawings
    52 Developing Visual Skills

Chapter Four: DRAWING AND SKETCHING INTERIOR ENVIRONMENTS
    61 Estimated One-Point Interior Perspective Drawings
    63 Estimated Two-Point Interior Perspective Drawings
    67 Refined Linear Perspective Methods
    68 Two-Point Plan Projection Method
    72 Prepared Perspective Grid Charts
    73 Perspectives Traced from Photographs
    76 Computer-Generated Imagery

Chapter Five: RENDERING

      81 **Introduction To Rendering**

      82 **Materials, Media, and Tools**

      90 **Rendering Orthographic Projection Drawings**

      97 **Rendering Perspective Drawings**

Chapter Six: SCALE MODELS

      109 **Introduction to Scale Models**

      110 **Materials and Tools**

      120 **Construction of Study Models**

Chapter Seven: PRESENTING MATERIALS AND FINISHES

      131 **Introduction to Materials Presentations**

      133 **Materials and Media**

      135 **Organization and Composition**

      141 **Basic Techniques**

Chapter Eight: PORTFOLIOS AND RESUMES

      147 **Graphic Design Components**

      150 **The Resume**

      162 **The Portfolio**

Appendix One: DIRECTORY OF PROFESSIONALS FEATURED

      169

Appendix Two: COLOR THEORY FOR RENDERING

      170

Appendix Three: SCALE FIGURES AND ENTOURAGE

      171

Appendix Four: FLOOR PLANS OF PROFESSIONAL CASE STUDY,
      173   SCIENCE MUSEUM OF MINNESOTA

Index

      175

Acknowledgments

This book is the work of many hands (and keyboards). It has been made possible by the generous contributions of numerous people to whom I would like to express my gratitude.

First, I must acknowledge my current and former students, who have taught me volumes and who give me the energy to keep going. I must thank all of the students who contributed work to this book, especially my current students Theresa Isaacson, Leanne Larson, Ardella Pieper, Cory Sherman, and Justin Thomson.

I have been amazed and touched by the generosity of members of the design community who shared time and contributed projects. Special thanks to my friend Lynn Barnhouse at Meyer, Scherer & Rockcastle Architects, who contributed a great deal of work and gave hours of her time. Thanks to Jane Rademacher at Ellerbe Becket, for all of her time and effort. Thanks also to Bob Albachten and Lisa Miller at Ellerbe Becket. And thank you to Thom Lasley of RSP Architects.

Jim Smart, of Smart Associates, contributed to this project on many levels, for which I am grateful. Thank you to Jim Moeller at Arthur Shuster Inc., Craig Beddow of Beddow Design, and Janet Lawson of Janet Lawson Architectural Illustration. Special thanks to Thomas Oliphant, and thank you to Aj Dumas of Mind's Eye Design.

I must acknowledge and thank my colleagues Tim O'Keeffe and Ben Pratt at the University of Wisconsin—Stout. Special thanks to Courtney Nystuen, a wonderful teacher and architect who contributed in many ways. It is also important to acknowledge the staff at Learning Technology Services—Marty Springer and Bill Wikrent—who provided a good deal of the photography included here.

Support from my parents and all of my family members has been extremely helpful throughout this long process. I must also acknowledge my long-ago family at Bruck Allen Architects in San Diego, which still informs the work I do—thanks for the memories. Finally, this project would not have been possible without Roger, a gem of a husband.

Introduction

The practice of interior design is complex and ever evolving. Technological and societal changes fueled by the industrial revolution and continued by more recent advancements in technology have shaped the profession in decisive ways. In a world that requires increasing professional specialization, interior design has gained recognition as an independent discipline. Work done by groundbreaking interior designers in the twentieth century has enhanced the built environment and increased the visibility of the profession. The development of educational standards, professional organizations, a qualifying exam, and legislative certification have increased the quality and credibility of practioners and fostered design excellence.

The design of interior environments requires specialized methods of presentation, and these are often overlooked in standard architecture texts. This book identifies methods used in the visual presentation of interior spaces and articulates them in written and visual language. Various phases of the design process are discussed in order to reveal the connection between process and presentation. Also, some basic principles of graphic design and portfolio design are discussed, because these areas are often overlooked.

The book is intended as a primer on interior design visual communication, with a range of styles and techniques presented. The goal is to provide information on visual presentation techniques and give students and practitioners a view of a variety of methods and materials. It is important to note that this book is not intended to impart ways of camouflaging poorly conceived design work with tricky techniques. This is not a rendering book as much as a portfolio of methods of communication. Good design deserves and requires adequate and appropriate methods of communication.

My desire to write this book grew from an ongoing pedagogical need: to show students a range of examples of presentation techniques and styles. Often design students look for the "right" way to create a presentation, and this is a mistake, because there are many ways of creating successful presentations. Interior design education has suffered from a lack of documentation of the many possible modes of presentation and a lack of specialized information for students. I have found that students exposed to a variety of methods and specific examples create appropriate and useful presentations, whereas students left uninformed about the possibilities often repeat the same lackluster or inappropriate type of presentation project after project.

Unlike those found in many books on rendering and presentation, most of the examples included here were executed by undergraduate design students. I've included these because I want students to see real examples of developing skills. It is important for all designers to develop drawing and sketching skills. Drawing and model building should not be reserved for the final presentation of fully developed designs. Instead, sketching, drawing, and model building must be seen as ways of seeing and exploring throughout the design process—from beginning to final presentation. I admit my desire to get interior designers to draw (and draw and draw). It is the best way to learn to visualize and do good work.

I have included some examples of work done by professional illustrators, digital illustrators, and model makers in order to demonstrate what is being done in current practice by specialists. The work is beautiful, highly professional, and depicts what top professionals produce. We can learn from this work, and perhaps allow it to influence our design drawings and in-process presentations.

The inclusion of some professional examples also allows practicing designers to view the work of their peers. Practicing designers rarely see presentations created by fellow practitioners (also known as competitors). I've also made an effort to focus on the work of designers in the Upper Middle West, specifically Minneapolis and Saint Paul, Minnesota, an area with a vibrant, helpful, dedicated design community often overlooked by national design publications.

Most chapters begin with information about specific materials and tools. Each chapter provides written instruction in the text as well as step-by-step illustrated instructions. In teaching, I've found some students learn best by reading and others by following brief graphic guides. My goal is to provide instruction for a variety of learning styles.

For the most part, this book covers conventional methods of drawing and presentation. The one exception is the material on perspective, where I have focused on estimated perspective sketching. Estimated sketching requires "eyeballing" perspectives; a method that I have found works well for students, although many educators find it horrifying! In addition to estimated sketching, information on more traditional methods of perspective drawing is included.

The examples and projects presented here range in scope from small residential student projects to huge public interior spaces designed by professionals. The projects range from purely decorative treatment of interior elements to space planning and interior architecture. It is important to note that several professional projects presented here are the work of architects involved in the design of interior space and exhibition design. This points to the overlap of the two professions, the breadth of current design practice, and some confusion over what the design of interior space should be called. When is it appropriate to use the term *interior architecture*? When *interior design*? Certainly that debate cannot be addressed in a book on presentation methods. In the book's title, I choose to use the term *interior design* because it describes the design of interior space, which is clearly a distinct area of specialization.

Orthographic Drawings

INTRODUCTION TO DRAWING

Interior design is a multifaceted and ever changing discipline. Currently, the practice of interior design, much like the rest of our lives, is in the midst of a technological revolution. Computers, the Internet, and fax machines have deeply influenced and changed the practice of design. For example, use of computer aided drafting and design (CADD) is fairly commonplace in current design practice, whereas ten years ago it was just beginning to gain in popularity.

In addition to undergoing rapid technological advancement, the profession of interior design has grown in terms of scope of work, specialization, and the range of design practiced. The growth of the profession, combined with efforts toward standards and licensing, have increased the legitimacy of interior design as a serious professional discipline.

These are significant changes that bring interior design, as a profession, to new heights and new challenges. Such change can be overwhelming and a bit frightening, and for that reason it is useful to consider the elements that remain constant in an evolving profession. In many ways, the design process itself remains constant—whether practiced with a stick in the sand, a technical pen, or a powerful new computer. There are many stories about designers drawing preliminary sketches on cocktail napkins or cheeseburger wrappers, and these stories lead us to a simple truth.

Professional designers conduct research, take piles of information, inspiration, and hard work and wrap them all together, in what is referred to as the design process, to create meaningful and useful environments. Whether design drawings are produced manually or by computer, they contain meaning that results in a finished product.

A constant and key factor in interior design is that human beings—and other living creatures—occupy and move within interior spaces. To create interior environments, professional designers must engage in a process that involves research, understanding, idea generation, evaluation, and documentation. These are significant constants that exist in a changing world.

For the most part, this book covers the process designers engage in and the related presentation techniques used in design communication. These processes and basic concepts are consistent, whether generated manually or by computer. Most of the examples included in this book were created manually, allowing students to learn the basics manually. However, most of the items described can currently be generated by computer. Regardless of how drawings and graphics are generated, they are part of a process of discovery, exploration, and creation.

This chapter covers what is often referred to as drafting as well as other forms of two-dimensional graphics. The term DRAFTING refers to measured drawings done with specialized tools and equipment. The truth is that not all drawings used in the process of interior design are drawn with the aid of tools. Often, those drawings created in the preliminary stages of the design process are rough sketches and involve little use of drafting tools or equipment. As designs are refined, there is clearly a need for highly accurate, measured, and detailed drawings, and these are drafted with tools.

This chapter presents the materials, equipment, and tools used for manually drafted and freehand design drawings, as well as an overview of the most common drawings used in interior design practice. The information presented in this chapter is meant as an overview, not a definitive drawing or drafting reference.

MATERIALS, TOOLS, AND EQUIPMENT

The graphics and drawings used in interior design practice vary, ranging from conceptual sketches and rough layouts to measured technical drawings. The materials, tools, and equipment used to create the variety of drawings and graphics are numerous and ever proliferating. The media and tools selected must be appropriate to the task at hand. This means that their proper selection requires careful consideration of the drawing type and use, as well as an understanding of the available products. Figure 1-1 illustrates commonly used drafting and drawing materials and equipment, as discussed in this chapter.

DRAWING SURFACES

The type of drawing surface selected directly affects the quality of the drawn image. Some surfaces accept pencil and ink readily and allow for clear, consistent imagery. Transparent papers allow for diazo reproduction (blueprinting) and can be used as an overlay to continue a drawing by transferring details from one sheet to another. Drawings produced on nontransparent surfaces must be reproduced by photocopying, photographic processes, or computer reproduction (scanning).

TRACING PAPER is the most common paper surface for sketching in-process design drawings and graphics. Known in various parts of the country as "trace," "flimsy," and "bumwad," this paper is highly transparent and relatively inexpensive. Tracing paper is available in cut sheets and in rolls in a variety of sizes. Rolls of tracing paper are best for interior design drawing because of the varying sizes of drawings required. Tracing paper is available in white, buff, and canary (yellow). Most designers have a personal preference, based on previous experience, as to color of tracing paper.

Because it is relatively inexpensive, tracing paper can be used to develop preliminary sketches and is often used for used for in-process drawings. This allows for exploration through the creation of many sketches and the generation of many ideas. Tracing paper also works very well overlaid on drawings for transfer and refinement of images. Often many layers of tracing paper are overlaid as a design is refined or as a complicated perspective drawing is constructed.

Figure 1-1

1. Compass		21. Dry cleaning pad
2. Architectural scales		22. Disposable ink pens
3. Drafting film		23. Technical pen
4. Template		24. Lead holder
5. T-Square		25. Lead pointer
6. Lettering triangle		26. Mechanical pencil
7. Triangle		27. Wooden graphite pencils
8. Appliqué film		28. Lay-out pencils
9. Vellum		29. Drafting brush
10. Tracing paper (roll)		
11. Cork backed ruler		
12. Flexible curve		
13. Drafting tape		
14. Drafting dots		
15. French curve		
16. French curve		
17. Adjustable triangle		
18. Electric eraser		
19. Eraser shield		
20. Erasers		

Images on tracing paper can be reproduced with the use of a diazo print machine and can be easily photocopied. However, tracing paper is very delicate and subject to tearing and crumpling. For this reason, it is not the best surface for any drawing that is to be extensively reproduced.

Most final design drawings and working drawings are drawn on **DRAFTING VELLUM**. Drafting vellum is a transparent paper that is available in a variety of finishes and weights (thicknesses) and is most often available in white. Drafting vellum should have a high rag or cotton content, giving it a rich finish, strength, and good stability. Vellum is excellent for line work generated with graphite pencils. Good quality diazo prints can be run from drafting vellum originals. Vellum is also photocopied, scanned, and photographed with excellent results.

In addition to vellum, **PLASTIC DRAFTING FILMS** are used for final drawings and for some design presentations. Plastic (and polyester) drafting films are expensive, tear resistant, and generally do not react to fluctuations in temperature or humidity (as do many paper surfaces). These films accept ink beautifully and allow for ink erasure rather easily. These films require the use of special pencils. Drafting film originals produce excellent diazo prints and photocopies. For years prior to the use of CADD, plastic film and ink drawings were considered the finest for reproduction. Drafting films have a special finish, on one or both sides, that allows for the use of ink and specialized pencils—this makes it different from untreated film and acetate sold for other purposes. Drafting films are durable, reproduce beautifully, and allow for the erasing of ink in most cases. They are not commonly used by students because of their cost and the need for specialized pencils.

ADHESIVE REPRODUCTION FILM, also called appliqué film and often referred to generically as "sticky back," is used on vellum or bond drawings. Typed or printed images can be drawn or photocopied onto adhesive reproduction film. The film is then carefully measured and cut and applied to the vellum or bond paper. Matte appliqué films accept pencil well; some types are repositionable but others are not. High-heat photocopiers may cause buckling of certain appliqué films; however, Rayven™ produces a variety of films for low-, medium-, and high-heat copiers.

Tracing paper, drafting vellum, and drafting film are commonly used in manual drawing in current professional practice. Nontransparent papers such as fine art drawing papers can be used with excellent results, yet they cannot be overlaid and do not reproduce well. The nature of the design process requires constant exploration and change, and transparent papers are well suited to this requirement.

Increasingly, design drawings are reproduced on large-format photocopying machines. In many firms and studios large bond paper copies have replaced "blueprints" as the preferred method of reproduction. Photocopiers have the advantage of printing from any paper surface (within reason), whereas diazo prints (blueprints) can be run only from drawings produced on transparent papers.

LINE- AND MARK-MAKING IMPLEMENTS

Lines and marks record spatial information in interior design drawings and graphics. Control of line thickness and the type of stroke used are important and convey specific information. Thus, the implement used to create lines and marks is a key factor in design drawing.

GRAPHITE is mixed with clay and other elements to produce what are commonly called "lead" pencils. Graphite pencils, used often in design drawing, are available in a range of hardness to softness, based on the mixture of clay to graphite. Graphite pencils and replaceable "leads" are coded with a standard rating system: H stands for hard; B stands for black (these are the softer leads). The number found next to the H or B refers to the level of hardness. For example, a 6B is softer than a B; an 8H is very hard indeed. F-rated leads are at the center of the range, and HB leads are slightly harder than Bs. The softer leads are used in sketching and rendering, whereas H, 2H, and, sometimes, F leads are most commonly used in drafting. Polymer-based leads, which are used on plastic and polyester drafting films, are often graded differently from graphite leads.

WOODEN DRAWING PENCILS have a graphite mixture encased in wood and are sharpened like standard wooden writing pencils. An electric sharpener is far superior to any other sharpening tool. Wooden drawing pencils are available in the full range of lead types.

MECHANICAL PENCILS are hollow instruments that hold very fine graphite leads. These are sold in a variety of lead widths to create a range of line weights. However, it is difficult to produce very bold lines with mechanical pencils. Because they have very fine leads, these pencils do not require sharpening. The leads of mechanical pencils snap and break easily under pressure and do not produce absolutely crisp lines.

LEAD HOLDERS are hollow implements that accept thicker leads than mechanical pencils. Although lead holders do not allow for any variety in lead widths, they do accept a range of lead types in terms of softness. Lead holders require the use of a specialized sharpener, known as a LEAD POINTER. Lead pointers can create a very sharp point and can help to create crisp, exacting lines. The relative thickness of the replaceable leads allows for drawing a range of line weights.

Specialized colored drafting pencils and leads can be used to develop drawings prior to hard-lining them. NON-PHOTO-BLUE colored pencils do not reproduce when photographed; however, they sometimes reproduce when photocopied. NONPRINT colored pencils do not reproduce in diazo prints. When appropriate, both types of pencil can be used to lay out drawings prior to completion.

One of the significant advantages of using graphite pencils is the ease of erasing. Most marks made with graphite leads can be erased to some degree. The harder leads are often the most difficult to erase because they are applied with pressure, which often leaves an indentation. Soft pencil marks are often lifted with gray kneaded erasers or pink erasers. Plastic and film erasers can be used to remove marks made with harder leads. A metal ERASER SHIELD is used to protect the drawing surface from unwanted erasing. DRY CLEANING PADS, containing art gum powder that sifts onto drawing surfaces, are available to keep drawings clean.

TECHNICAL PENS have tubular points and refillable ink reservoirs. They are available in a range of point sizes that allow for absolute control of line weight. Because they employ black ink and metal points, technical pens create the finest line work of any drawing implement. Technical pens must be used with the appropriate ink, as specified by the manufacturer. The tips of some pens—especially the finer tips—can clog, causing disaster. In addition, technical pens require proper cleaning and maintenance, which includes keeping the points screwed in properly, placing the caps firmly on the pens, and storing the pens upright.

DISPOSABLE TECHNICAL PENS combine a tubular support with a felt tip. These are available in a range of point sizes. These pens require no maintenance or cleaning, making them easy to use. Although disposable pens have been known to skip, causing inconsistent line work, they have improved a great deal recently and are becoming very popular.

FELT-TIP PENS are available in a range of styles and point sizes; they are often used in sketching, exploration, and rendering. Felt-tip pens are not generally used for refined drafted drawings or working drawings.

Erasing ink marks is rather difficult and requires special erasers. Hard plastic erasers can remove ink. However, an **ELECTRIC ERASER** with the appropriate eraser insert is most useful in removing ink. Electric erasers are very effective but must always be used with an eraser shield. Ink marks on film are erased more easily than those on vellum. Sharp razor blades are sometimes used to scrape ink away from drawing surfaces.

A quality **DRAWING BOARD** is required for the creation of successful drawings. Serious students must purchase a top-quality drawing board if possible. The board should accommodate a minimum paper size of 24 by 36 inches. Drawing boards should be covered with a specialized vinyl drawing surface, sold at drafting and art supply stores. The vinyl surface helps to improve line consistency.

T SQUARES are used in conjunction with the edge of the drawing board to provide an accurate horizontal line or right angle for drawings. The more expensive **PARALLEL RULERS** can be attached to drawing boards using a system of screws, cables, and pulleys. This creates the sliding straightedge that is the standard in professional practice. Triangles are used with a T square to create vertical and angled lines. Adjustable and 45/45 degree and 30/60 degree triangles are readily available. Triangles should be fairly clear, easy to see through, and as substantial as possible. An inking triangle with raised edges is required when using ink. It is also useful to have a tiny triangle on hand as an aid in lettering. Triangles should never be used as a cutting edge; this will ruin them. A cork-backed metal ruler is the best edge for cutting.

DRAFTING TAPE or **PRECUT DRAFTING DOTS** are used to attach drawings to drawing boards. Unlike standard masking and household tape, drafting tape and dots are very easy to remove from both the paper and the drawing board. A **DRAFTING BRUSH** is used to remove eraser debris from the drawing surface.

Measured interior design drawings require the use of a proportional scale. This allows for large areas to be reduced in size to fit on relatively small drawings. An **ARCHITECTURAL SCALE** is the standard scale ruler used in interior design drawing. Architectural scales are marked in a manner that makes measuring in scale fairly easy. For example, in 1/4-inch scale, the ruler is marked so that each 1/4 inch measures 1 foot in scale. Architectural scales have inches marked below the zero marking; these are used to measure elements that are not exact to the foot. In transferring measurements, great care should be taken to record accurate dimensions. Scale rulers should never be used to draw against, as this will result in poorly drawn lines and damaged scale rulers.

TEMPLATES are most commonly constructed of plastic and are used much like stencils to draw various shapes, including circles, ellipses, furnishings, and fixtures. The more expensive templates, constructed of heavy, durable plastic, are worth the extra money. Furniture and fixture templates work well to quickly lay out and plan spaces.

However, in presentation drawings furniture and fixtures drawn from templates can appear artificial and monotonous.

FRENCH CURVES are drawn against as an aid in drawing curved lines. FLEXIBLE CURVES, also known as snakes, are also used as an aid in drawing curved lines. Flexible curves have flexible splines that can be bent to accommodate the desired curve. These also work well for transferring curves from one drawing surface to another. A compass is used for drawing accurate circles and arcs. A COMPASS is useful in situations where a template does not contain a circle of the required size. It is worthwhile to purchase a good compass that adjusts easily and accepts drawing leads and ink heads.

UNDERSTANDING ORTHOGRAPHIC PROJECTION DRAWINGS

The practice of interior design requires the creation and use of various types of drawings. These can be divided into three very broad categories based on purpose. The first type of drawing allows the designer to explore ideas (known as ideation) and work conceptually. The second type allows the designer to communicate to members of the design team, the client, end users, consultants, and other professionals (these are presentation drawings). The third type of drawing conveys the technical information required for construction (these drawings are referred to as construction documents or working drawings). This book has as its focus the first two types of drawing, those used for exploration and presentation or graphic communication of ideas.

Unlike ideation sketches, presentation drawings and construction documents must use certain standard drawing conventions in order to clearly communicate and delineate the proposed design. Unlike fine art drawing, design drawing requires adherence to conventions, proportional scale, and accuracy of line. Design drawings are highly standardized so that they carry universal meaning. Or, as one early reviewer of this book put it, "Design drawing is much like a language; the drawings must convey the designer's meaning clearly."

The design drawings most commonly used in scaled delineation of interior environments are floor plans, interior elevations, sections, and reflected ceiling plans. These drawings, called ORTHOGRAPHIC PROJECTIONS, are created by projecting information about an object onto an imaginary plane known as the PICTURE PLANE. This direct projection of an object's dimensions allows for orthographic projections to retain shape and proportion, making these drawings accurate and precise. Orthographic projection creates fragmentary views of an object, resulting in the need for multiple drawings. This means that, because of their fragmentary nature, orthographic projections become parts of a system and are mutually dependent on one another. By their nature, orthographic projections appear flat and lack the three-dimensional quality of perspective drawings. One way to visualize

Figure 1-2
When an object is enclosed in a glass box, each plane of the box can serve as a picture plane.

Figure 1-3
The view through the top plane (picture plane) creates a plan view, in this case a roof plan.

Figure 1-4
The view through the picture plane enclosing the side of the box is called an elevation.

Figure 1-5
A section is a view of an object with the picture plane slicing neatly through it.
Drawings by Justin Thomson.

orthographic projection is to imagine an object enclosed in a transparent box. Each transparent plane of the enclosing box serves as the picture plane for that face of the object (Figure 1-2).

The view through the top plane of the enclosing box is called a PLAN. In a plan view only those elements seen when looking directly down at the object are drawn. Figure 1-3 depicts a roof plan.

The views through the picture planes that form the sides of the enclosing box are called ELEVATIONS. Elevations depict only what is visible when viewed directly through the picture plane (Figure 1-4).

A SECTION portrays a view of the object or building with a vertical plane sliced through it and removed. One way of understanding section views is to imagine that a very sharp plane has been inserted into the object or building, cutting neatly into it and revealing the structure and complexity of the object's form (Figure 1-5).

ORTHOGRAPHIC PROJECTION DRAWINGS FOR INTERIOR ENVIRONMENTS

The special orthographic projection drawings used in delineation of interior environments are based on the concepts mentioned to this point. These drawings impart information particular to interior construction.

FLOOR PLANS

A FLOOR PLAN is a view as though looking straight down at a room or building after a horizontal cut has been made through the structure. A floor plan can also be called a HORIZONTAL BUILDING SECTION, because the drawing is created by cutting through the building horizontally at roughly four to five feet above floor level and removing the top half. With the building cut open and viewed from above, important information such as wall, door, and window locations can be drawn to scale (Figure 1-6). Additional design elements such as fixtures and furniture can be drawn in appropriate locations to scale in a floor plan.

In the United States floor plans are most often drawn at a scale of 1/8″ = 1′-0″ or 1/4″ = 1′-0″; although this varies according to project conditions. Larger-scale floor plans are useful for presentation of complex or highly detailed spaces. Smaller-scale floor plans are required for large projects and are also used as key plans in complex presentations.

In drawing floor plans, it is important to convey significant spatial relationships with consistent graphic conventions. Various line weights are used to convey depths and qualities of form. In standard floor plans the boldest line weight is used to outline those elements that have been cut through and are closest to the viewer (such as full-height wall lines). An intermediate line weight is employed to outline objects that lie below the plane of the cut but above the floor plane, such as fix-

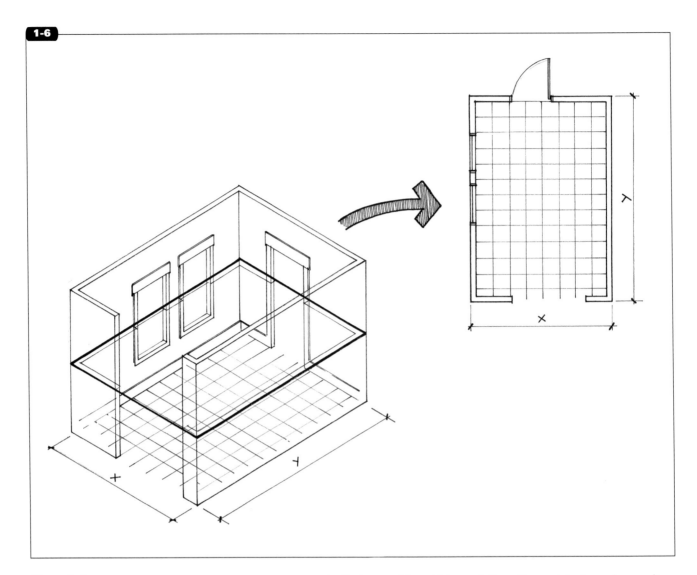

Figure 1-6
A floor plan is created when the picture plane cuts through the building horizontally, at 4′ to 5′ above floor level.

tures, built-ins, and furnishings. A finer line weight is used to outline surface treatment of the floors and other horizontal planes such as tile and wood grain. Objects that are hidden, such as shelves, or above the plane of the cut are dashed or ghosted in; this must be done in a manner that is consistent throughout the presentation.

Figures 1-7a and 1-7b are examples of town house floor plans drawn by hand and employing standard conventions and reference symbols.

Standard doors are generally drawn open at 90 degrees to the wall and are often shown with the arc of their swing. The door frame and the space it requires must be considered in the drawing of the door system (this means the dimensions of the frame must be considered). Windowsills are typically outlined, often with a lighter line weight at the sill only. Window frames and sheets of glass are shown in various detail as scale allows. Stairs are generally shown as broken off past the height of the plane of the cut; this is signified with a special cutline. An arrow should be included, indicating the direction of the stairs from the level of the floor plan, with the word UP or DOWN (DN.) adjacent to the directional arrow.

Figure 1-7a

Town house lower-level floor plan employing standard drafting conventions.

1. Boldest lines indicate the location of cut, meaning full-height walls are bold.

2. Fixtures, cabinetry, and finish materials are drawn with progressively lighter lines as they recede from the cut location.

3. Elements that are above or below the cutline (such as cabinets and soffits) are indicated with dashed lines.

4. Standard doors are drawn open at 90 degrees with the arc of swing shown.

5. Specialized doors such as bifold doors, sliding doors, and pocket doors are drawn in a way that indicates size and construction.

6. Window glass and sill lines are shown, often with a lighter-weight line than walls.

7. Stairs are drawn as broken off past the line of the cut. A special cutline is used. An arrow indicating direction from the level of the plan and the word "up" or "down" (dn.) are included.

8. A title, North arrow, and scale notation are required on all plans. Because this drawing was reduced, a standard written scale was omitted; instead, a graphic scale device is included.

9. This is a section reference symbol. The arrow indicates the direction of the view of the section. The letter indicates the particular drawing on sheet A2 that is referenced.

10. This is an elevation reference symbol. The arrow indicates the direction of the view of the elevation. The number indicates the particular drawing on sheet A3 that is referenced.

11. This is a centerline, indicating the centerline of the shared wall in the town house.

Design by Courtney Nystuen.

UPPER LEVEL PLAN

0   2   4   8

1-7b

Figure 1-7b

Town house upper-level floor plan employing standard drafting conventions.

1. Boldest lines indicate the location of cut, meaning full-height walls are bold.

2. Fixtures, cabinetry, and finish materials are drawn with progressively lighter lines as they recede from the cut location.

3. Elements that are above or below the cutline (such as cabinets and soffits) are indicated with dashed lines.

4. Standard doors are drawn open at 90 degrees with the arc of swing shown.

5. Specialized doors such as bifold doors, sliding doors, and pocket doors are drawn in a way that indicates size and construction.

6. Window glass and sill lines are shown, often in a with a lighter-weight line than walls.

7. Stairs are drawn as broken off past the line of the cut. A special cutline is used. An arrow indicating direction from the level of the plan and the word "up" or "down" (dn.) are included.

8. A title, North arrow, and scale notation are required on all plans. Because this drawing was reduced, a standard written scale was omitted; instead, a graphic scale device is included.

9. This is a section reference symbol. The arrow indicates the direction of the view of the section. The letter indicates the particular drawing on sheet A2 that is referenced.

10. This is a centerline, indicating the centerline of the shared wall in the town house.

Design by Courtney Nystuen.

A title, a North arrow, and some type of scale notation should be included on all floor plans. Scale notation can be stated numerically, for example: $1/4''=1'-0''$. Current practice often requires the use of a graphic scaling device, which allows for reduction, enlargement, and electronic transmission of the drawings.

Symbols relating the floor plan to additional orthographic views or details are often drawn on the floor plan and serve as cross-references.

Successful floor plan presentation drawings require a thorough understanding of drafting conventions. Presentation floor plans may be drawn very fastidiously with tools or drawn freehand. Regardless of the style of drawing, presentation floor plans must be accurate and drawn to the appropriate scale so that they communicate the design and can be used by the designer as the project moves forward. Presentation floor plans are enhanced by the use of tone, value, color, and/or other graphic devices. The graphic enhancement of floor plans is discussed in greater detail in Chapter 5.

INTERIOR ELEVATIONS

Just as exterior elevations are created to reveal exterior elements and features, interior elevations reveal the interior features of a building. One way to understand the creation of interior elevations is to imagine ourselves inside the room we are drawing. Imagine standing inside a room facing one wall directly, with a large sheet of glass (the picture plane) inserted between the viewer and the wall. The interior elevation can then be created by outlining (projecting onto the picture plane) the significant features of the wall. Each wall of the room can be drawn in elevation by means of projecting what is visible as the viewer faces that wall directly (Figure 1-8).

Interior elevations are used extensively in professional practice. Successful elevations must clearly depict all interior architectural elements in a consistent scale. Interior elevations are typically drawn in a scale ranging from $1/4'' = 1'-0''$ to $1'' = 1'-0''$. Elevations drawn to depict accessories, equipment, cabinetry, fixtures, and design details are often drawn at $3/8'' = 1'-0''$ or $1/2'' = 1'-0''$. Millwork and other highly complicated elevations are often drawn at $1/2'' = 1'-0''$ or larger.

All elevations require the use of differing line weights to clearly communicate spatial relationships. Typically, any portion of walls cut through and those closest to the viewer are drawn using a bold line weight. Receding elements become progressively lighter in line weight as they move farther from the picture plane. Some designers draw the line representing the ground line as the boldest line, with the lines representing the top and sides of the wall drawn just slightly lighter in weight. Figure 1-9 depicts kitchen elevations for the town house project.

Interior elevations can be difficult for beginning students to master. However, they deserve a student's full attention because accurate elevations are necessary to successfully communicate key elements of a design. Like floor plans, elevations used for design presentations vary greatly from those used for construction. Elevations used for construction drawings must necessarily contain significant dimensions as well as appropriate technical information. Elevations used for presentations can be drawn more freely and often contain less technical information, but must be drawn accurately and in consistent scale.

For elevations to work well in visual presentations, they must be clearly keyed, noted, or referenced to the floor plan. Regardless of the referencing method used, titles must be included beneath all elevations and scale should be noted.

Elevations used for presentations are enhanced by the use of tone, value, color, and/or other graphic devices, many of which are discussed in Chapter 5.

1-8

Figure 1-8
In drawing interior elevations, the picture plane is inserted between the viewer and wall(s). What is visible through the picture plane is drawn in elevation.

1-9

① ELEVATION
④
|0 |2 |4

② ELEVATION
④
|0 |2 |4

Figure 1-9
Interior elevations for the townhouse project.
1. Portions of walls cut into or closest to viewer are bold.
2. Receding elements are drawn with progressively lighter lines.
3. In elevations including cabinetry and or millwork, details such as countertops, door frames, and hardware should be included.
4. Interior elevations require titles, reference symbols (names or numbers), and scale notation.

Design by Courtney Nystuen.

SECTIONS

As described earlier, a building section is a view of a building created as though a vertical plane has cut through the building and been removed. Unlike interior elevations, which depict only what occurs inside the interior, sections can expose the structure of the building. In drawing sections, it is important to include the outline of the structural elements as well as the internal configuration of the interior space. Sections require varied line weights as a means of describing depths and spatial relationships. It is typical to show what is cut through, and therefore closest to the viewer, in the boldest line weight; receding features and details are drawn using progressively lighter line weights.

It is important to consider carefully the most useful location (or locations) of the building to show in section. The section should be cut through the building as a single continuous plane. Sections should expose and convey important interior relationships and details such as doors, windows, changes in floor level, ceiling heights, and, in some cases, finish material locations.

Design and presentation sections differ greatly from construction sections. Construction sections require technical information in order to communicate information about building systems. In contrast, design sections and presentation sections focus on form, finish materials, and definition of interior space. For sections to work well in visual presentations, they must be clearly keyed, noted, or referenced to the appropriate floor plan. Generally, sections are referenced to the floor plan with use of a symbol that denotes the locations of the vertical cut. Figure 1-10 is an example of a hand-drawn design section for the town house project.

REFLECTED CEILING PLANS

REFLECTED CEILING PLANS are often used in conjunction with floor plans, elevations, and sections to communicate interior design. Reflected ceiling plans communicate important information about the design of the ceiling, such as materials, layout and locations of fixtures, and ceiling heights. A reflected ceiling plan is drawn as though a giant mirror were on the floor, reflecting the elements located on the ceiling. The use of reflective imagery allows for the ceiling plan to have exactly the same orientation as the floor plan.

There is often a distinction between ceiling plans used for presentation and those used for construction. Typically, ceilings plans created for construction are highly technical and include a great deal of information. Reflected ceiling plans used in design presentations can be simplified. Most often reflected ceiling plans used in presentations include simplified lighting information, ceiling heights, and finish materials, whereas precisely measured, complex technical lighting plans are required for construction. Figure 1-11 is a simple reflected ceiling plan for the town house project appropriate for use in a design presentation.

Together, floor plans, elevations, sections, and ceiling plans communicate information about the quality of an interior environment. Because these drawings are abstracted, fragmented versions

Ⓐ SECTION
③ |0 |2 |4 |8

Figure 1-10

Building section for the town house project.

1. Boldest lines indicate location of cut.
2. Receding elements are drawn with progressively lighter lines.
3. Sections require titles, reference symbols (names or numbers), and scale notation.

Design by Courtney Nystuen.

of three-dimensional form, they depend on one another to communicate effectively.

The orthographic projections covered in this chapter relate directly to the communication and design of interior space. Differing versions of orthographic projections are used for construction and presentation, but they are used in one form or another on virtually all projects.

Additional types of orthographic drawings are used to communicate the features of buildings and building sites. Site plans, foundation plans, demolition plans, roof plans, framing plans, exterior elevations, wall sections, and design details are also used in the design of buildings. Designers of interior space must be knowledgeable about the nature of these drawings, how they are created, and how they relate to the interior architecture of a building.

LETTERING

Traditionally, floor plans, elevations, and sections contained notes and dimensions written in a standardized style of hand lettering. However, recent changes in technology allow for creation of type that can be applied to hand-drawn orthographic projections. Lettering and type can be computer generated, printed on adhesive reproduction film ("sticky back"), and applied to drawings. Lettering is also created

REFLECTED CEILING PLAN

by specialized machines (lettering machines) that print on adhesive-backed tape that can be applied to drawings. Lettering machines can be used to produce type in a range of sizes, styles, and colors. In addition, CADD allows for consistent, standardized type to be readily applied to the appropriate location on a drawing.

Even with these changes in technology, it is useful to develop the ability to hand letter in a consistent, standardized style. Many designers still create presentation drawings by hand, and for the sake of visual consistency, hand lettering is crucial. Hand lettering is also often used on quick sketches, design details, and for dimensions and revisions of drawings.

There are some basic rules for lettering design drawings, as well as some stylistic elements that influence letter form. Guidelines are required for all lettering locations. Horizontal guidelines create the lines on which the lettering rests. Consistent spacing between the lines of lettering is required. Vertical guidelines must be drawn so that the lines of type are aligned consistently. Lettering for design drawings is typically all capitals, allowing all letters to fit within a single pair of guidelines, with no tips or tails above or below the guidelines. Letters should have perfectly vertical strokes; the vertical strokes should not slant to the left or to the right. A tiny lettering triangle is used as a straightedge in making vertical strokes.

Figure 1-11

Simple reflected ceiling plan for town house project.

1. Ceiling heights are noted and enclosed in a symbol.
2. Light fixture locations are noted with various symbols and are keyed to a legend.
3. Finish materials such as gypsum board, wood, and ceiling tiles are indicated in scale.
4. Reflected ceiling plans require titles, North arrows, and scale notation.

Design by Courtney Nystuen.

HAND LETTERING BASICS

HORIZONTAL AND VERTICAL GUIDELINES ARE REQUIRED FOR ACCURATE AND CONSISTENT HAND LETTERING.

USE ALL CAPITAL LETTERS, WITH NO STEMS BELOW OR ABOVE GUIDELINES.

VERTICAL STROKES (STEMS) SHOULD BE PERFECTLY VERTICAL AND NOT SLANTED.
USE A SMALL TRIANGLE AS A GUIDE IN CREATING PERFECT VERTICALS.

MOST LETTERS HAVE A SQUARE SHAPE 'A' 'B' 'C' 'D' 'E'

SPACE BETWEEN LETTERS IS MINIMAL AND IS VISUALLY ASSESSED, NOT MEASURED WITH RULERS.

AN 'O' OR "C" SIZE SPACE SHOULD BE LEFT BETWEEN WORDS, LEAVE A SLIGHTLY LARGER SPACE BETWEEN SENTENCES

TYPICALLY VERTICALS ARE THIN WHILE HORIZONTAL STROKES ARE THICK. THIS IS DONE IN PENCIL BY CREATING A CHISEL POINT AND ROLLING THE PENCIL FROM THE THIN TO THICK SIDE.

THE BEGINNING AND END OF EACH LETTER STROKE CAN BE EMPHASIZED TO INCREASE LEGIBILITY. STROKES SHOULD LOOK LIKE THIS: BEGIN ——————————— END

WHILE INDIVIDUAL LETTERING STYLES VARY, CONSISTENCY MUST BE MAINTAINED WITHIN THE DOCUMENT OR DRAWING.

THE FOLLOWING ARE HAND LETTERING STYLES THAT VARY SLIGHTLY:

A B C D E F G H I J K L M N O P Q R S T U V W X Y Z
1 2 3 4 5 6 7 8 9 10
A B C D E F G H I J K L M N O P Q R S T U V W X Y Z
1 2 3 4 5 6 7 8 9 10
A B C D E F G H I J K L M N O P Q R S T U V W X Y Z 1 2 3 4 5 6 7 8 9 10

1-12

Figure 1-12
Hand lettering reference.

Currently, popular lettering form calls for block letters that are square in shape and wide, rather than narrow. Letter spacing is not equally measured between letters. Instead, the letters in a word are rather tightly packed together and are "eyeballed" for overall uniformity of spacing. An O- or C-sized space should be left between words. For the most part, lettering should be laid out in blocks and should contain no indentations.

Many designers prefer a lettering style in which the vertical or downstroke of a letter is very thin and crisp and the horizontal is bold. It is also common to emphasize the beginning and end of each stroke. Figure 1-12 is a hand lettering reference.

DIMENSIONS

Dimensions, required on all construction drawings, are sometimes required on drawings used for presentation purposes. Their inclusion is based on the project and the presentation audience. Dimensions must be accurate, complete, and readable. Horizontal dimensions should read across the sheet from left to right. Vertical dimensions must read from the left hand edge so as not to require rotating the drawing in a variety of directions.

Dimension lines should be of a thin, crisp line weight that sets them apart from wall and other construction lines. The lines leading from the area dimensioned to the dimension lines (known as leader lines) should be spaced slightly apart from construction lines.

Dimensions should be written above the dimension lines, so that they are underlined by the dimension lines. Dimensions are best written in feet and inches. For example, 2′-4″ is written, not 28″. The single exception is made for items measuring less than one foot; these are listed in inches only. Figure 1-13 is a floor plan using standard dimensioning conventions.

COMPUTER AIDED DRAFTING AND DESIGN (CADD)

The descriptions of orthographic drawings to this point have included examples that were drafted by the human hand. Most designers currently use a computer as a design tool, as an aid in the creation of orthographic drawings, and in design presentations. It is important to note that the conceptual basis for orthographic drawings and drafting conventions is the same whether created by hand or through the use of electronic tools. The meaning communicated in a floor plan is the

Figure 1-13

Dimensioned upper-level floor plan for town house project.

1. Dimension lines should be light and crisp.
2. Horizontal written dimensions sit above the dimension lines and read left to right.
3. Vertical written dimensions sit above the dimension lines and read from left.
4. Leader lines run from the building location being dimensioned to the dimension lines. Leader lines should not touch the building; instead, they should be drawn slightly away.
5. Dimensions are written in feet and inches unless less than one foot.
6. Dimensions measured from centerlines must be clearly indicated. Windows and doors are commonly measured to centerlines. Design by Courtney Nystuen.

⊕ LOWER LEVEL PLAN

1-14a

Figure 1-14a
Town house lower-level
floor plan drawn with
AutoCAD R 12™.
Design by Courtney Nystuen.
Drawing by Theresa Isaacson

same whether the drawing is created by hand or with the use of CADD. Figures 1-14a and 1-14b are floor plans of the town house project generated on AutoCAD R12™.

CADD is used with increasing popularity by architects, designers, and engineers. Reliability, flexibility, accuracy, clarity, and speed are some of the reasons that CADD has been embraced by the broader design community. Graduates of architecture and design programs are currently expected to have an understanding of CADD as well as familiarity with additional computer-generated imagery and information. CADD software used in the production of orthographic drawings ranges a great deal in price and sophistication. Currently, the debate about the "best" CADD software rages on.

Professional use of CADD in various phases of the design process is commonplace and ever expanding. Some practicing designers still do a great deal of hand drafting. Many designers begin the design of a project drawing by hand and proceed to the use of CADD with preliminary design sketches. Increasingly, designers use CADD from the onset of a project and generate all design drawings and construction documents using computers.

(ROOF)

DN

(OPEN)

UPPER LEVEL PLAN

1-14b

Figure 1-14b
Town house upper-level floor plan
drawn with AutoCAD R 12™.
Design by Courtney Nystuen.
Drawing by Theresa Isaacson.

REFERENCES
Ching, Frank. *Architectural Graphics*. New York: John Wiley & Sons, 1996.

Ching, Frank. *A Visual Dictionary of Architecture*. New York: John Wiley & Sons, 1995.

Forseth, Kevin, and David Vaughn. *Graphics for Architecture*. New York: John Wiley & Sons, 1998.

Liebling, Ralph. *Architectural Working Drawings*. New York: John Wiley & Sons, 1990.

Porter, Tom. *Architectural Drawing*. New York: Van Nostrand Reinhold, 1990.

Smith, C. Ray. *Interior Design in 20th Century America: A History*. New York: Harper & Row, 1987.

C h a p t e r **2**

The Design Process
And Related Graphics

INTRODUCTION TO THE DESIGN PROCESS

The complexity of the design process requires that at various points along the way, designers must communicate aspects and outcomes of the process to clients and consultants. Like professionals, students must present in-process projects to team members, instructors, and guest critics. Visual presentations must vary to accommodate the process of design and to communicate both process and outcome.

Writing in *Interior Design Illustrated*, Francis Ching identifies three basic stages of design process: analysis, synthesis, and evaluation. According to Ching, analysis involves defining and understanding the problem; synthesis involves the formulation of possible solutions; and evaluation involves a critical review of the strengths and weaknesses of the proposed solutions.

Interestingly, these three basic stages of design process are used by design practitioners in a variety of disciplines. Industrial designers, graphic designers, exhibition designers, and others often engage in a similar process. Of course, the design disciplines vary a great deal in terms of professional practice and final outcome. For this reason, actual interior design process and project phases are quite distinct and are more elaborate than the three basic stages may indicate.

For purposes of contractual organization, the process of design engaged in by architects and interior designers in the United States has been divided into five basic project phases: (1) PROGRAMMING, (2) SCHEMATIC DESIGN, (3) DESIGN DEVELOPMENT, (4) CONSTRUCTION DOCUMENTATION, and (5) CONTRACT ADMINISTRATION. These phases are derived from the American Institute of Architects' (AIA) Owner-Architect Agreement for Interior Design Services© and the American Society of Interior Designers' (ASID) Interior Design Services Agreement©. Both of these documents serve as contracts for design services and are reflective of the current design process and project management in the United States. Figure 2-1 is a description of design phases and related visual presentation methods.

Peña, Parshall, and Kelly, writing in *Problem Seeking,* identify the actual design process as taking place in the first three project phases. They state that "programming is part of the total design process but is separate from schematic design." The authors go on to link schematic design and design development as the second and third phases of the total design process. The following sections are intended as an exploration of the three phases of the design process identified by Peña, Parshall, Kelly, and others and as a study of the drawings and graphics used to communicate, document, inform, and clarify the work done during these phases.

Project Phase	Typical Tasks and Activities	Typical Means of Visual Presentation
Programming also known as pre-design	<u>In depth analysis and documentation of needs, requirements goals and objectives.</u> Can include: identification of space and adjacency requirements analysis; asset assessment; specialized needs assessments; codes and accessibility research and identification of conceptual and thematic issues. As well as; analysis of architectural or site parameters; and analysis of scheduling and budget.	Most often written information compiled in a programming report. Often includes problem identification, diagrams, charts, matrixes, and may include some orthographic drawings and early fit studies. May include preliminary scheduling graphics.
Schematic Design also known as the preliminary *design* phase	<u>Preliminary conceptual, spatial, conceptual, and technical design of project.</u> Includes preliminary space planning often using; relationship diagrams; matrices; bubble diagrams; blocking diagrams; stacking plans; and fit plans. As well as initial furnishings, fixtures and equipment design/layout. Development of project's conceptual and thematic issues. Color, material and finish studies. Preliminary code review. Preliminary budgetary information.	Graphic presentation of preliminary design; can include relationship diagrams; blocking and fit plans; preliminary space plan(s); preliminary furnishing and equipment layouts; preliminary elevations and sections; preliminary 3-D drawings; preliminary color and materials studies; and study models. Presentation may also include graphic presentation of conceptual and thematic issues using sketches, diagrams, and mixed media.
Design Development	<u>Refinement of finalized design.</u> Includes space plan and design of interior construction elements and details. Often involves incorporation of lighting, electrical, plumbing, and mechanical systems design; as well as data and telecommunication systems integration. Often includes millwork design and detailing. Also includes color, materials, and finish selection. Design and specification of furnishings, fixtures, and equipment, as well as refinement of budgetary and scheduling information.	Finalized, refined design presentation incorporating all necessary components of design. Graphic presentation of finalized design can include conceptual diagrams; space plan(s); and plan(s) for furnishings, fixtures and equipment, as well as elevations; sections; ceiling plans; 3-D drawings; colors, materials, and finish samples; scale models and mockups. Multimedia presentations can incorporate all of the above elements plus sound and animation.
Construction Documents	<u>Preparation of drafted, working drawings and/or contract documents.</u> Includes preparation of drawings, schedules, details, and specifications, as well as coordination and integration of consultant's documents. Can include preparation of specialized equipment and/or furnishings documents for bidding by purchasing agents. May include purchasing documents.	Preparation of contract documents. Often includes submission to general contractor(s) and purchasing agents for bid and to appropriate agencies for plan check.
Construction Administration	<u>Guide and review construction and installation.</u> Can include periodic site visits and creation of progress reports. Coordination and review of shop drawings and sample submittals. May include clarification and interpretation of drawings, as well as possible review of billing and payment. Preparation of punch list. May include move coordination and supervision of furnishings, fixtures and equipment installation.	Communication with contractors, agencies and clients is primarily written and verbal. May include scheduling, budgetary, and administrative graphics.

Adapted from: AIA Owner-Architect Agreement for Interior Design Services© and the ASID Interior Design Services Agreement©.

2-1

PROGRAMMING

The experienced, creative designer withholds judgment, resists preconceived solutions and the pressure to synthesize until all the information is in. He refuses to make sketches until he knows the client's problem....programming is the prelude to good design. (Peña, Parshall, and Kelly, 1987).

Programming, also known as predesign or strategic planning, involves detailed analysis of the client's (or end user's) needs, requirements, goals, budgetary factors, and assets, as well as analysis of architectural or site parameters and constraints. Information gathered about the user's needs and requirements is often documented in written form, whereas architectural or site parameters are often communicated graphically through orthographic projection. These two distinct forms of communication, verbal and graphic, must be brought together in the early stages of design.

Some firms employ professionals who work as programmers and then hand the project over to designers. It is also common for project managers and/or designers to work on project programming and then continue to work on the design or management of the project. It could be said that programmers and designers are separate specialists, given the distinctions between programming (analysis) and design (synthesis). However, many firms and designers choose

Figure 2-1
Project phases and related visual presentation methods.

not to separate these specialties or do so only on very large or pro-gramming-intensive projects.

In practice, programming varies greatly from project to project. This is due to variation in project type and size and to the quantity and quality of information supplied by the client (or end user). In some cases clients provide designers with highly detailed written programs. In other situations clients begin with little more than general information or simply exclaim, "We need more space, we are growing very fast" or "Help, we are out of control." In situations such as the latter, research and detective work must be done to create programming information that will allow for the creation of success-ful design solutions.

It is difficult to distill the programming process used in a variety of projects into a brief summary. Clearly, the programming required for a major metropolitan public library is very different from that required in a small-scale residential renovation. It is important, there-fore, to consider what *all* projects relating to interior environments share in terms of programming.

All projects require careful analysis of space requirements for current and future needs, as well as analysis of work processes, adjacen-cy requirements, and organizational structure (or life-style and needs assessment factors in residential design). Physical inventories and asset assessments are required to evaluate existing furniture and equipment as well as to plan for future needs. Building code, accessibility, and health/safety factors must also be researched as part of the programming process.

In addition to this primarily quantitative information, there are aesthetic requirements. Cultural and psychological aspects of the project must also be identified by the designers. All of these should be researched and can be documented in a programming report that is reviewed by the client and used by the project design team. When possible, it is important to include a problem statement with the programming report. The problem statement is a concise identifica-tion of key issues, limitations, objectives, and goals that allow for a clearer understanding of the project. With the programming report complete, the designers can begin the job of synthesis and the design process continues.

Residential projects generally present less need for intensive programming graphics. Programming is a significant element of the residential design process; however, the relationships, adjacencies, and organization of the space are often simplified in relation to large commercial and public spaces. For this reason the discussion to fol-low focuses primarily on commercial design where a significant amount of visual communication of programming information is often required.

Clients, consultants, and designers require graphic analysis as a way of understanding programming data and information. Diagrams, charts, matrices, and visual imagery are comprehended with greater ease than pages of written documentation. It is useful

ECO TOYS   PROGRAMMING INFORMATION

COMPANY HISTORY:
Eco Toys is a young, dynamic company. Larry Leader, the company president started the company in 1985. The company designs and produces toys for preschoolers, using recycled plastic products. Eco Toys has enjoyed tremendous success and growth in the last five years. Owing to recent growth, the company must move to larger, better-organized design and marketing offices.

COMPANY STRUCTURE AND ORGANIZATION:
The president is at the center of all company operations and constantly interacts with all members of his staff. Mr. Leader depends a great deal on his assistant Steve Stable. Although Mr. Leader is in touch with all levels of operation, he has set up the company in a horizontal organizational structure. This means that all members of the Eco Toys staff have equal status and power and are seen as important contributors to the organization. The design of the space should reflect the organizational structure of the company.

GENERAL REQUIREMENTS:
Because of the non hierarchical organizational structure, all workstations must be exactly the same size. As a means of encouraging team meetings and sharing within departments small (8' x 8') individual workstations have been requested. As a result of complicated egress conditions, the existing door locations must be retained.

DEPARTMENT INFORMATION AND REQUIREMENTS:

ENTRY/RECEPTION: Very public must visually represent company's mission. Requires reception desk with work surface and transaction counter, task seating. Guest seating for 6. Must allow space for movement of children into toy test center. Must be near conference room, toy test center and close to marketing dept.

CONFERENCE ROOM: Very public and attractive, seating for 10 at tables with additional seating available. Requires multimedia center. View if possible. Immediately adjacent to toy test center (with visual connection), close to reception, and near marketing dept.

TOY TESTING CENTER: Open and flexible space for use by 4 - 6 preschool age children. Must be visually connected to conference room and adjacent to entry and conference room.

DESIGN DEPT.: 2 designers and 2 assistants. All individual work spaces must accommodate CADD station, plus layout space, 2 file drawers, and handy reference storage. Adjacent to model shop -- a messy, noisy, enclosed space ~120 sq. ft. min. Adjacent to engineering dept. Nearby team meeting space with casual seating for 4. room for plotter, display area, and filing.

MARKETING DEPT.: 2 marketing managers and 1 assistant. All individual work spaces must accommodate a P.C., 2 file drawers, and handy reference storage. Must have adjacent team space with table and seating for 5. Must be near conference room, toy test and reception area.

ENGINEERING DEPT.: 2 engineers. All individual work spaces must accommodate CADD station, and lay-out space, two file drawers, and handy reference storage. Must be adjacent to design dept. and near design team space.

ACCOUNTING DEPT.: 2 accountants. Individual work spaces must accommodate a P.C. and printer, 2 file drawers, and handy reference storage. Requires some privacy and no major interaction with other departments, with the exception of the President.

PRESIDENT: Pres. plus assistant (2 total); must accommodate P.C. and printer, 2 file drawers, and handy reference storage. President to have small conference table (to seat 4). Near all depts. and break room.

BREAK ROOM: Generous counter space, base and wall cabinets, sink, refrigerator, microwave, and commercial coffee makers. Seating for 8 minimum.

COPY/MAIL: Room for copy machine and adjacent 5 lineal ft. of collating space, room for 16 mailboxes, paper, and supply storage. Convenient to corridor.

STORAGE: Generous heavy-duty shelving. Must be enclosed and private, requires shelving and ventilation for Local Area Computer Network.

2-2a

to develop ways of sorting and simplifying programming information so that it can be easily assimilated.

Successful graphic communication of both the programming process and the programming report can help to create useful information from overwhelming mounds of raw data. A sample project created to illustrate the drawings and graphics used in the various phases of the design project is referenced throughout this chapter. Figure 2-2a contains written programming information regarding the sample project. Figure 2-2b is a floor plan indicating the given architectural parameters of the project.

2-2b

PROGRAMMING ANALYSIS GRAPHICS

Many designers find it useful to obtain early programming data and incorporate it into graphic worksheets. Using a flip chart pad, brown kraft paper, or other heavy paper, the programmers can create large easy-to-read graphic documents. These sheets are created so that they may be easily understood by the client and can therefore be approved or commented on. Often the eventual project designers find these sheets useful as a means of project documentation.

Figure 2-2a
Programming information for the sample project.

Figure 2-2b
Floor plan for the sample project.
By Leanne Larson.

Figure 2-3

Examples of programming analysis graphics for the sample project.

The book *Problem Seeking* (Peña, Parshall, and Kelly, 1987) provides an additional technique for the graphic recording of information generated in the early stages of programming, using a device known as analysis cards. Analysis cards allow for easy comprehension, discussion, clarification, and feedback. The cards are drawn from interview notes and early programming data. Based on the notion that visual information is more easily comprehended than verbal, the cards contain simple graphic imagery with few words and concise messages. The cards are most successful if they are large enough for use in a wall display or presentation and if they are reduced to very simple but specific information. Figure 2-3 illustrates program analysis graphics for a sample project. See Figure C-6 for a color version of a programming analysis graphic.

PROGRAMMING MATRICES

Matrices are extremely useful tools in programming, incorporating a wealth of information into an easily comprehended visual tool. An adjacency matrix is commonly used as a means of visually documenting spatial proximity, identifying related activities and services, and establishing priorities. Adjacency matrices vary in complexity in relation to project requirements. Large-scale, complex projects often

Figure 2-4
Simple adjacency matrix for the sample project.

ECO TOYS

	RECEPTION	CONFERENCE	TOY TEST	PRES.	DESIGN	MARKETING	ENGINEERING	ACCOUNTING	MODEL SHOP	BREAK	COPY/MAIL	STORAGE
RECEPTION	·	●	●	O	O	◑	O	O	X	O	O	O
CONFERENCE	●	·	●	O	O	◑	O	O	X	O	O	O
TOY TEST	●	●	·	O	O	◑	O	O	X	O	O	O
PRES.	O	O	O	·	◑	◑	◑	◑	O	◑	O	O
DESIGN	O	O	O	◑	·	O	◑	O	●	O	O	O
MARKETING	◑	◑	◑	◑	O	·	O	O	O	O	O	O
ENGINEERING	O	O	O	◑	◑	O	·	O	O	O	O	O
ACCOUNTING	O	O	O	◑	O	O	O	·	O	O	O	O
MODEL SHOP	X	X	X	O	●	O	O	O	·	O	O	O
BREAK	O	O	O	◑	O	O	O	O	O	·	O	O
COPY/MAIL	O	O	O	O	O	O	O	O	O	O	·	◎
STORAGE	O	O	O	O	O	O	O	O	O	O	◎	·

LEGEND
● MAJOR ADJACENCY
◑ MINOR ADJACENCY
O NOT CLOSELY RELATED
X UNDESIRABLE

Figure 2-5
Another type of adjacency matrix for the sample project.

require highly detailed adjacency matrices. Figures 2-4 and 2-5 illustrate two types of adjacency matrix.

A criteria matrix can distill project issues such as needs for privacy, natural light, and security into a concise, consistent format. Large-scale, complex design projects may require numerous detailed, complex matrices, and smaller, less complex projects require more simplified matrices. Criteria matrices are used in residential design projects and in the programming of public spaces. Smaller projects allow for criteria matrices to be combined with adjacency matrices. Figure 2-6 illustrates a criteria matrix that includes adjacency information. Special types of matrices are used by designers on particular projects.

Programming graphics, such as project worksheets, analysis cards, and a variety of matrices, are widely used in interior design practice. These are presented to the client or end user for comment, clarification, and approval. Many of these graphics are refined, corrected, and improved upon during the programming process and are eventually included in the final programming report.

	ECO TOYS	Adjacencies	# of Dept Members	Seating Req's	Public Access	Privacy	Plumbing	Data/Phone	Special Req's	Comments
1	Reception	② ③ 6	1	6 min	●			●	Y	Visually rep mission; used by adults & children; "dynamic & playful"
2	Conference	① ③ 6		10+	●			●	Y	"Dynamic & playful"; multimedia center; multiple lap-top /computers
3	Toy Test	① ②		4-6	●			○	Y	Used by preschoolers;.open, flexible, playful
4	President	5 6 7 8 10	2	4				●	Y	PC, printer, 2 file drawers, ref storage for each 8' x 8' work space
5	Design	⑨ ⑦	4	4 min				●	Y	CADD, lay-out, 2 file drawers, ref storage for each 8' x 8' work space
6	Marketing	① ② 3	3	5 min				●	Y	PC, printer, 2 file drawers, ref storage for each 8' x 8' work space
7	Engineering	⑤	2					●	Y	CADD, lay-out, 2 file drawers, ref storage for each 8' x 8' work space
8	Accounting	4	2			●		●	Y	PC, printer, 2 file drawers, ref storage for each 8' x 8' work space
9	Model Shop	⑤			○	●	○		Y	Messy & noisy; enclosed
10	Break Room	4		8 min			●	○	Y	Relaxing & inviting; gen counters; refrig, microwave, sink, coffee makers req
11	Copy/Mail							○	Y	5 lineal feet collating space; 16 mailboxes; storage
12	Storage					●			Y	Generous heavy-duty shelving; ventilation

Legend

①	Major Adjacency	○	Secondary Requirement
1	Minor Adjacency	Y	Yes, See Comments
●	Mandatory Requirement	X	Undesirable

2-6

SCHEMATIC DESIGN

With the programming phase completed, designers may begin the work of synthesis. Another way of stating this is that with the problem clearly *stated*, the problem *solving* can begin. The creation of relationship diagrams is often a first step in the schematic design of a project. Relationship diagrams serve a variety of functions that allow the designers to digest and internalize the programming information. Relationship diagrams also allow the designer to begin to use graphics to come to terms with the physical qualities of the project.

One type of relationship diagram explores the relationship of functional areas to one another and uses information completed on the criteria and adjacency matrices. This type of one-step diagram can be adequate for smaller commercial and residential projects. Larger-scale, complex projects often require a series of relationship diagrams. Diagrams of this type do not generally relate to architectural or site parameters and are not drawn to scale. Most specialized or complex projects require additional diagrams that explore issues such as personal interaction, flexibility, and privacy requirements.

BUBBLE DIAGRAMS

As relationship diagrams begin to incorporate and account for necessary requirements and adjacencies, they can become refined into what are generally referred to as BUBBLE DIAGRAMS. Bubble diagrams take the project one step further in the schematic design process. Often bubble diagrams relate approximately to the actual architectural parameters (the building space) in rough scale. In addition, they often incorporate elements identified in criteria and adjacency matrices through the use of graphic devices keyed to a legend. Figures 2-7a, 2-7b, 2-7c, 2-7d, and 2-7e are a sequence of bubble diagrams for the sample project. See Figure C-7 for a color version of a bubble diagram.

It is important to note that a primary purpose of these early schematic diagrams is to generate a number of options. Brainstorming many ideas is highly advisable. Designers with years of experience use brainstorming techniques, as should students of design. Successful design requires sparks of creativity in every phase, and these sparks are fostered by nurturing idea generation. Rarely does the first try (or the first several) create a masterpiece or a workable solution. It is often the combination of several diverse schemes that eventually generates a good solution.

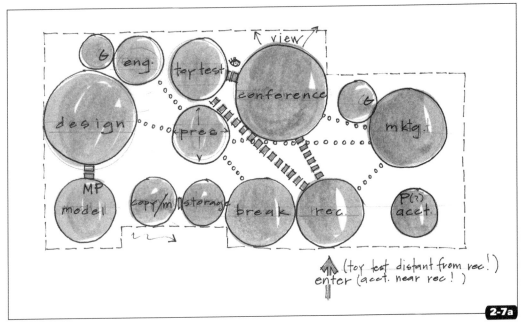

Figures 2-7a, 2-7b, 2-7c, 2-7d
Bubble diagrams for the sample project.

2-7b

2-7c

2-7d

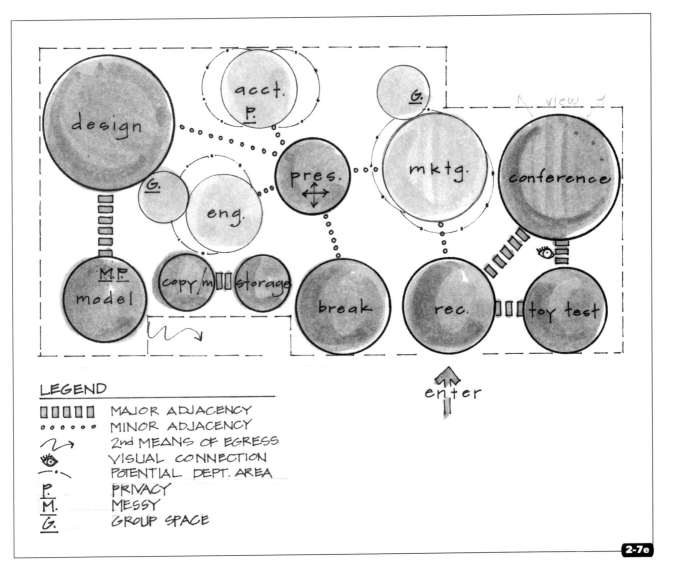

LEGEND

▯▯▯▯▯	MAJOR ADJACENCY
• • • • • •	MINOR ADJACENCY
⌇→	2nd MEANS OF EGRESS
👁	VISUAL CONNECTION
—·—·—	POTENTIAL DEPT. AREA
P.	PRIVACY
M.	MESSY
G.	GROUP SPACE

2-7e

BLOCKING DIAGRAMS

Bubble diagrams are part of a continuous process of refinement. One diagram may have useful components that can be combined with elements of another. As this process of refinement continues, designers often proceed to BLOCKING DIAGRAMS.

Before moving to blocking diagrams, design students benefit from the creation of space studies, also known as area prototype sketches. Each area or function is sketched in scale with furniture and equipment included, and these sketches can be used for purposes of approximation in the blocking diagram. Space study sketches are also helpful in the design of systems furniture, allowing students to explore possibilities and gain insight into the use of these products. See Figures 2-8a, 2-8b, and 2-8c for examples of space studies.

Blocking diagrams are usually generated on tracing paper taped over a scaled, drafted floor plan of the existing or proposed building. In rare cases projects do not involve the use of existing architectural parameters, because the interior space will dictate the final building form. In these cases, bubble diagrams and blocking plans are some-

Figure 2-7e
Final, successful bubble diagram for the sample project.

Figures 2-8a, 2-8b, 2-8c

Space studies for the sample project.

ECO TOYS
SPACE STUDIES

COPY/MAIL STORAGE MODEL SHOP TOY TEST

KITCHEN/BREAK RECEPTION CONFERENCE

2-8a

2-8b

ECO TOYS
WORK STATION STUDIES

+ PANEL CREEP or wall thickness

high interaction / limited privacy.

+ PANEL CREEP or wall thickness

high interaction / some privacy
limited work surface area.

+ PANEL CREEP or wall thickness

high privacy / limited interaction

ECO TOYS
GROUP SPACE STUDIES

DESIGN: "LIVING RM"

MARKETING: "PUZZLE TABLE"

PRES.: "LIVING RM"

DESIGN: "COMBINATION"

MARKETING: "ROUND PLUG IN"

PRES.: "LIVING RM 2"

DESIGN "PUZZLE TABLE"

MARKETING "RECT. PLUG IN"

PRES.: "TRADITIONAL"

2-8c

times the genesis for the eventual building plan. It is increasingly common for designers to begin the blocking plan process on CADD and take the project through the rest of the design process using CADD.

As stated, blocking diagrams are generally drawn to scale and relate directly to the architectural parameters or the existing building plan. Blocking plans are generally drawn with each area or function represented by a block of the appropriate square footage; circulation areas are often blocked in as rectilinear corridors. Figures 2-9a, 2-9b, and 2-9c are blocking diagrams.

Some experienced designers move quickly to blocking diagrams, forgoing the use of bubble diagrams, whereas others dislike the blocky, confining nature of blocking diagrams. Many designers develop a personal system of schematic diagrams that is a combination of bubble and blocking diagrams. The approach and graphic quality of schematic diagrams used by individual designers vary greatly, yet the underlying purpose is consistent. Designers use these diagrams to move from verbal and simplified graphic notation toward true scale and the eventual realization of architectural form.

FIT PLANS AND STACKING PLANS

A FIT PLAN can be considered a further refinement of the blocking diagram. Basically, the fit plan is a test determining whether the requirements and needs clarified in programming "fit" into a given space. In some cases, fit plans are drawn up when a client reviews a piece of real

**Figures 2-9a,
2-9b, 2-9c**

Blocking diagrams for the sample project. Note that these blocking diagrams focus on the layout of individual work spaces.

estate or a potential site. In other cases, fit plans are drawn up to indicate the way a proposed office tower may eventually be laid out. These types of fit plans are generated for both real estate professionals and end users.

In still other situations the fit plan is part of the final stage of the space-planning process. For this reason, fit plans often contain furniture and equipment accurately drawn to scale as a means of testing the space plan for fit and for client review.

A STACKING PLAN is used when a project occupies more than one floor of a building. Often the interrelationships of departments or work group locations are examined in a stacking diagram. Generally, stacking diagrams are created early in the design process as a means of evaluating the use of each floor before refined space planning is done.

CONCEPTUAL DESIGN

The schematic design phase is often a time when designers explore symbolic representation for the conceptual foundation of a project. Although relationship, bubble, and blocking diagrams represent functional and spatial requirements, they sometimes do little to illuminate the conceptual nature of a project. It is often useful to employ an abstract diagram or graphic device to represent the conceptual qualities of a project.

One means of illustrating conceptual project themes is the use of a design PARTI. Frank Ching, writing in *A Visual Dictionary of Architecture* (1995), defines a parti as "the basic scheme or concept for an architectural design represented by a diagram." A design parti can take a wide range of forms, from a highly simplified graphic symbol to a more complex plan diagram. Some designers use a conceptual diagram such as a parti as an aid in bringing together the functional and conceptual components of a design. The parti, or another conceptual diagram, can be used throughout the design process as a conceptual anchor for the project. Designers sometimes employ the parti extensively, and it may be the foundation for the design and appear as a logo or project icon on all presentation graphics.

A formal design parti is not sought for all design projects. Most projects do, however, include a considerable number of thematic issues. Views, geography, climate, building context and site, functional requirements, and cultural issues may contribute to the project on a conceptual level. Often the existing building form provides project constraints in the design of interior environments. Most designers find it useful to articulate and explore conceptual and thematic issues early in the schematic phase of a project. The methods of presentation of conceptual components of a project are varied and highly personal and involve both verbal and graphic notations.

For purposes of organization, space planning and conceptual development are discussed separately here. However, in design practice these elements are brought together in the early stages of project design. Bubble diagrams often incorporate conceptual elements, and a design parti can serve as an organizational anchor in the space-planning process. It is important to see the schematic/conceptual design phases as a continuous process of refinement whereby all elements are brought together. Figures 2-10a, 2-10b, and 2-10c are conceptual sketches that might be generated during the drawing of blocking diagrams.

The hand-drawn floor plan sketch contains the following handwritten labels: flooring, ceiling canopy, conf., display, flooring, model, copy/m. stor., break, rec, toy test, president in "center" as pinwheel.

2-10c

SCHEMATIC DESIGN PRESENTATION GRAPHICS

The preliminary design(s) created in this process of refinement must be evaluated by the designer or design team, as well the client, in order for the project to continue. Presentation of the preliminary design may be casual or formal, depending on the nature of the project. In all cases it is useful to consider the purpose of the presentation as well as its audience. The audience for a preliminary presentation may include the client, consultants, real estate professionals, and those with financial interests in the project. Prior to the creation of any presentation, it is worthwhile to take time to assess the audience for the presentation, because identifying and understanding this audience is imperative.

In addressing members of the design team or design consultants, a presentation may consist of rough sketches and multiple layers of paper. Designers and most consultants are familiar with orthographic drawings and can wade through some confusing and messy drawings and notes. Many clients, however, require easy-to-understand graphic images as a means to understanding the schematic presentation. The client must understand the preliminary design in order to evaluate and approve it, which is necessary for the project to continue successfully.

The preliminary client presentation must communicate the underlying project research and the constraints that have led to the preliminary design. These include preliminary budgetary information, preliminary scheduling information, research of appropriate building codes, and programming information. Generally, at a minimum, the preliminary schematic design presentation requires a floor plan as a means of communicating the space plan. When the project involves more than one floor, each floor plan and stacking plans are typically included in the preliminary presentation.

Figure 2-11
Schematic presentation for the
sample project, ink on vellum.

The preliminary presentation floor plan(s) may be drawn freely, drafted with tools, or generated on CADD. Regardless of the means of drawing or drafting, the floor plan should be drawn to scale and include a North arrow and titles. If the designers wish to communicate several design schemes, the various floor plans must be clearly labeled with some sort of notation system, such as "Scheme 1" or "Concept 1."

Some preliminary presentations include programming information, floor plans, and minimal additional graphics, whereas other projects require preliminary presentations that include additional drawings such as elevations, sections, and preliminary perspective drawings, as well as models and materials samples. The following chapters cover some of these additional forms of preliminary presentation. A successful presentation of the preliminary schematic design communicates information to the client and other interested parties and allows for input, comments, criticism, and approval. Figure 2-11 is an example of a schematic design presentation for the sample project and is based on issues covered to this point. Figure 2-12 is a student schematic design presentation of the sample projects. Figures 2-13a and 2-13b are examples of a professional schematic design presentation.

Most often, designers come away from a preliminary presentation with lists of suggestions from the client. These range from minor corrections or clarifications to major changes in functional, conceptual, or aesthetic aspects of the design.

Figure 2-12
Student schematic presentation
for the sample project (images
photocopied onto plastic,
mounted on foam board).
By Roderick Sauskojus.

The information generated by feedback to the first schematic presentation allows the designers to move forward in the refinement of the design. Depending on project requirements and constraints and the number of changes requested by the client, more schematic presentations may be required. It is common for smaller, less complicated projects to receive quick general approval, allowing the designers to move forward in the design process. Larger projects can require many additional meetings and presentations before the client grants approval of the schematic design.

In interviewing designers, I have found great variety in the formality, visual quality, and the quantity of information included in preliminary design presentations. Clearly, there is a range of styles of presentation and firms have varying standards. Even with this great variety, there seem to be elements of consistency. Most designers describe a need to communicate very clearly in early presentations and to make sure that the client understands the elements of the design presented. Most also describe the importance of making clear the very preliminary nature of the design. Many designers find that clients

Figure 2-13a
Professional schematic design
presentation, ink and graphite
on vellum and bond paper.
By Bruck Allen Architects Inc.
Project team: Christopher Allen,
Mark Bausback, Brian Church,
and Randall Rhoads.

need time to settle into ideas; thus, pinning things down too early can be frightening and frustrating for them.

DESIGN DEVELOPMENT

The design development of a project involves finalizing the space plan and fully developing all of the components of the design. All

VIEW FROM LOBBY

MAIN AXIS VIEW

VIEW FROM MEZZANINE
CONFERENCE ROOMS

VIEW FROM MANUFACTURING

2-13b

aspects of the design must come together and be resolved in this phase of the project. It is useful for students to know that the goal is to have the design of a project completed in the design development phase. It is important to keep in mind that the phase following design development is construction documentation, which involves preparation of the project for construction. In large firms the project is often handed from the design team to the production team upon completion of design development.

In a perfect world, every detail would be considered and resolved in the design development phase of a project. For the most part, design development drawings are drafted accurately and to scale. Some designers create design development drawings that are somewhat sketchy, and others create extremely precise, highly detailed drawings. In either case, the entire volume of a space must be explored and refined to ensure a successful design project and to allow for a smooth transition into the construction documentation phase of the project.

The presentation made upon the completion of the design development phase is often seen as the comprehensive final design presentation of a project. This presentation must include every possible element of the design to ensure clear communication of the final design. Orthographic drawings, including detailed floor plans, ceiling plans, detailed elevations, sections, and design details, are generally part of the presentation. In addition, technical drawings, millwork drawings and samples, materials samples, and furnishings and fixtures samples and images are often included in the final design development presentation.

Smaller projects often move quickly from schematic to design development and involve minimal presentations. More complex projects require many interim presentations and meetings. Weekly or biweekly design meetings are not uncommon on large or complex projects. Final design presentations vary enormously because of the variety of projects and working styles of designers. Clearly, there is no existing industry standard for the preparation of design development presentations. It is with pride and sometimes secrecy that firms and designers create successful presentations.

Although design presentations reflect the concerns, aesthetics, and tastes of designer(s) and client, communication is the one constant in the preparation of design presentations. The final design presentation must clearly communicate the elements of the design. For the project to move forward, the design must be understood and approved by the client. In addition to the client or end user, a wide range of individuals may have to review and approve of the design.

Projects dependent on public funding, such as libraries and municipal buildings, often require public review of the design. Many projects require design approval of municipal agencies or local community groups. Investors and consultants must often review design presentations before a project can move forward. All of these individuals form the eventual audience for the design presentation, and understanding this audience is a key to the successful communication of the design.

The following chapters offer information on additional visual devices employed in the design and presentation of projects. These are discussed separately for purposes of clarity, but all are used throughout the design process as a means of exploring and communicating the design.

REFERENCES

Ballast, David. *Interior Design Reference Manual.* Belmont, CA: Professional Publications, 1995.

Ching, Frank. *A Visual Dictionary of Architecture.* New York: John Wiley & Sons, 1995.

Ching, Francis. *Interior Design Illustrated.* New York: John Wiley & Sons, 1987.

Harwood, Bouie. "An Interior Design Experience Program, Part II: Developing the Experiences." *Journal of Interior Design* 22(1), 1531.

Henley, Pamela. *Interior Design Practicum Exam Workbook.* Belmont, CA: Professional Publications, 1995.

Karlen, Mark. *Space Planning Basics.* New York: Van Nostrand Reinhold, 1993.

Koberg, Don, and Jim Bagnall. *The Universal Traveler.* Menlo Park, CA: Crisp Publications, 1991.

Peña, William, Steven Parshall, and Kevin Kelly. *Problem Seeking.* Washington, DC: AIA Press, 1987.

Paraline and Perspective Drawings

INTRODUCTION TO
THREE-DIMENSIONAL VIEWS

Perspective and paraline drawings differ greatly from orthographic drawings. Both perspective and paraline drawings offer a more natural view of space. It is important to note that these three-dimensional views (also known as pictorial drawings) are useful at every phase of the design process. Pictorial drawings work well in the various phases of the design process as a method of examining and refining ideas and should not be reserved merely as a means of final project presentation.

The purpose of this chapter is to present a wide range of three-dimensional drawing methods and procedures. These methods range from freehand sketches to measured, hard-lined perspective illustrations. Students of design should seek a method or methods that work well for them as individuals. The goal, then, is to find drawing methods that are useful as tools throughout the design process and to realize that pictorial drawing is a way of seeing, useful for all designers.

Unlike orthographic projections, three-dimensional views allow for a single depiction of a large portion of an interior space. This type of drawing can also permit clients to clearly understand the design of a project. In addition, three-dimensional views of a space allow the designer to *see* and *explore* the entire volume of space and make design decisions accordingly.

Many designers create paraline and perspective drawings by hand, but computers are increasingly used for the generation of perspective drawings. Some designers state that they can explore the total volume of a space only when drawing it in perspective by hand. Many designers have mentioned that they use a combination of hand sketching and computer-generated perspective imagery.

Some designers use computer-generated imagery from the inception of a project and create no hand drawings at any point in the design process. Increasingly, design graduates are expected to have the ability to create three-dimensional views both by hand and with the use of computers.

Paraline and perspective drawings are created as line drawings and used as such in presentations, or are rendered upon completion. Some perspective and paraline line drawings work very well in communicating a design to an audience without the addition of value or color rendering. This is especially true if additional descriptive items such as material and finish samples are also used in the presentation. Therefore, it is worthwhile to attempt to generate descriptive line drawings that communicate a design successfully and to see rendering as a secondary step in the drawing process.

The tools and materials used in perspective and paraline drawings are very similar to those used in orthographic projection drawings and the other forms of graphic communication mentioned previously. An abundance of tracing paper is probably the most important material in the production of perspective drawings. The transparency and low cost of tracing paper make it highly useful as a visualization tool. As soon as a drawing becomes confusing to sort out, a new sheet of tracing paper can be overlaid! When tracing paper is used as an overlay, a variety of colored pencils can be used as a visual aid in the construction of three-dimensional drawings.

Pencils and pens can both work well in the construction of three dimensional views. Although the choice of implements is highly personal, quick-sketching methods are best accomplished with marking pens that provide quick visual impact. Marking pens also eliminate the use of erasers—this actually helps with visualization. This approach is tough at first, but worth the effort.

Refined-measured paraline and perspective drawings are most often constructed in pencil on tracing paper, with many layers of paper and a variety of colored pencils used. These drawings often require the use of drafting tools but are also drawn freehand by some individuals. The final hard-lined, measured paraline or perspective line drawing is often done on high-quality vellum or drafting film with drafting pencils or ink pens. This allows for the line drawing to be reproduced by a variety of reprographic methods on a variety of papers. Once reproduced, the drawing may be incorporated into a presentation with or without rendering. Information on rendering and reprographics is available in Chapter 5.

PARALINE DRAWINGS

PARALINE DRAWINGS are quick, accurate, and useful in the communication of interior form. The method of construction of these drawings is based on the relationship of three principal axes (x, y, and z). Although there are several types of paraline drawings, all share common characteristics: (1) paraline drawings have parallel lines drawn as parallel, and lines do not converge to vanishing points, (2) vertical lines are drawn as true verticals in paraline drawings, and (3) paraline drawings are drawn using some method of proportional scale.

PLAN OBLIQUE DRAWINGS

One type of paraline drawing commonly used in the communication of interior environments is known as a PLAN OBLIQUE. Figure 3-1 provides a quick reference of plan oblique construction. Plan obliques can be constructed quickly, because they are drawn by projecting directly off the floor plan. Drawing a plan oblique requires the rotation of the floor plan to appropriate angles as measured against a horizontal baseline. The most common angles of plan rotation or orientation are 30 degrees—60 degrees, and 45

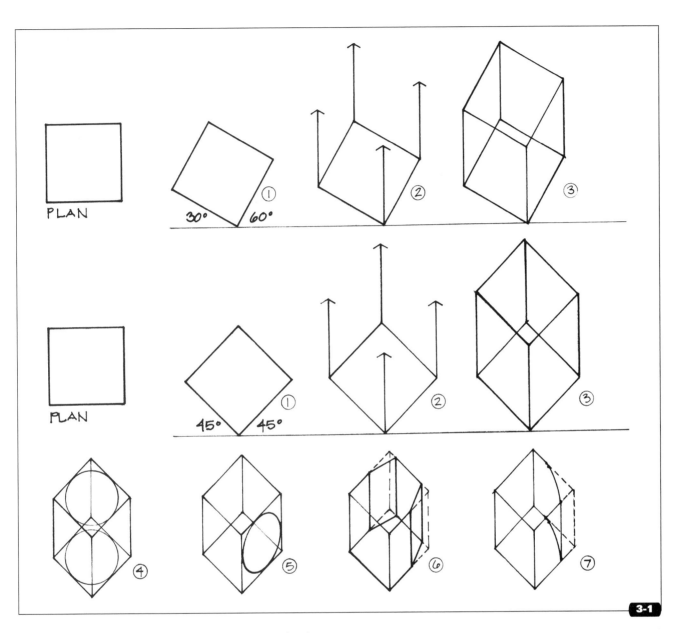

PLAN

30° 60° ① ② ③

PLAN

45° 45° ① ② ③

④ ⑤ ⑥ ⑦

3-1

degrees—45 degrees, although plan obliques may be drawn at any two angles that together equal 90 degrees. Vertical elements are drawn by projecting locations vertically from the plan to the appropriate height. Horizontal elements are drawn using the same angles as those used in the orientation of the plan.

Because they are generally projected from existing plans, these drawings are created quickly and can be used throughout the design process as an aid in seeing and understanding the environment. The angle of rotation changes the orientation of the drawing and must be considered in the construction of these drawings. The angle of rotation used allows for varying views and emphasis on particular portions of the space. Often plan obliques employ some method of visual elimination of portions of walls in order to depict the space successfully. This is often done by cutaway views or by ghosting in portions of walls.

Circles and curvilinear forms can be drawn in plan obliques

Figure 3-1

Quick reference: plan oblique construction.

1. Rotate scaled plan to appropriate angles (shown here 30 degrees/60 degrees and 45 degrees/45degrees).

2. Draw vertical lines upward to appropriate height in scale.

3. Lines parallel to the base plane (the floor plan) are drawn at the same angles as plan.

4. Circles found on the plan and its parallel planes are drawn as circles.

5. Circles found on vertical planes are drawn as ellipses.

6. Create an enclosing box to measure and locate onaxonometric lines.

7. Create an enclosing box to measure and plot irregular and curvilinear lines and planes.

Figure 3-2
A plan oblique drawing of a
residential storage area.

using a number of methods. Circles found in the true size planes on plan oblique drawings retain their true size and form. This means that a true circle found in a plan (and on surfaces parallel to the plan) remains a true circle in a plan oblique. Circles or curvilinear lines found on the vertical, nonfrontal planes (those drawn at angles extending from the plan) appear as ellipses. (For additional information on ellipse construction see Figures 3-14 and 3-15.)

The location of free-form curvilinear lines can be approximated by plotting locations on the plan and extending them vertically to the appropriate height. Curvilinear forms found on nonfrontal planes can be approximated using a grid to plot locations and transferring them to the appropriate location of a grided area on the oblique drawing.

Objects or lines that are not parallel to any of the three primary axes are not measurable in scale and can be tricky to draw. To draw nonaxonometric lines and objects, an enclosing box can be created within the axonometric framework. The enclosing box can provide measuring lines with which to locate the end points of the object lines. Nonaxonometric lines that are parallel to one another remain parallel in plan oblique drawings.

3-2

60°   30°

Figure 3-3
A plan oblique drawing of
the Eco Toys project (see
Chapter 2).

Plan oblique drawings are very quick to create and are useful as an aid in the design process. However, although they are a simple and effective means of visualization for the designer, they can be confusing for clients who are not accustomed to viewing this type of drawing. Figures 3-2 and 3-3 are examples of plan oblique drawings.

ISOMETRIC DRAWINGS

An **isometric** is a paraline drawing based on the use of 30-degree angles. Unlike plan obliques, isometrics cannot be constructed by simple rotation and projection of the plan. Instead, the drawing of an isometric requires the reconstruction of the plan in scale with the two ground plane axes (x and y axes) at 30 degrees. All elements that are parallel to the ground plane are drawn at 30 degrees. As in other types of paraline drawings, vertical elements remain vertical in isometric drawings. Scale measurements can be made along any of the three principal axes (x, y, and z). Figure 3-4 provides a quick reference of isometric construction.

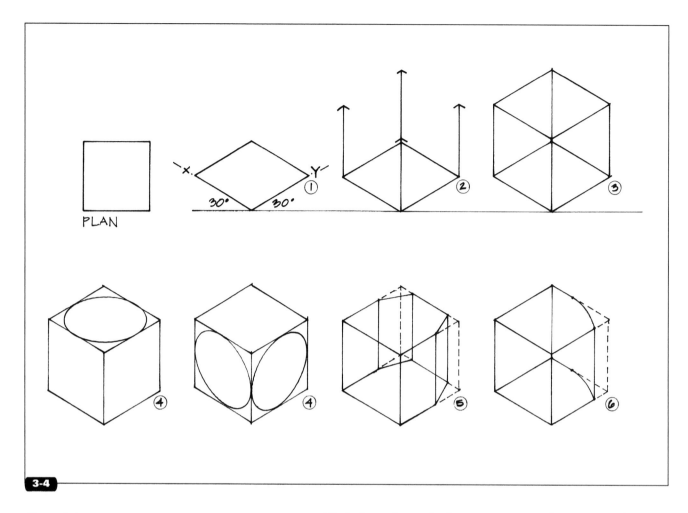

Figure 3-4
Quick reference: isometric construction.

1. Redraw plan, in scale, with x and y axes at 30 degrees.
2. Draw vertical lines upward to appropriate height in scale.
3. Lines parallel to the x and y axes are drawn at the same angles as plan.
4. All circles are drawn as ellipses in an isometric drawing.
5. Create an enclosing box to measure and locate nonaxonometric lines.
6. Create an enclosing box to measure and plot irregular and curvilinear lines and planes.

All circles and circular lines in isometric drawings are drawn as ellipses. Isometric ellipse templates can be used in isometric drawing. For additional information on ellipse construction, see Figures 3-14 and 3-15. Lines not parallel to the three principal axes are created by using an enclosing box method with which to locate the object. Isometric drawings offer a very balanced view and the least distortion of any paraline drawing.

Isometric drawings can be used at any phase of the design process as a means of communicating form and spatial relationships. Isometrics are also used in technical and construction documents. Although isometrics offer some advantages, they are time-consuming, somewhat inflexible, and do not emphasize any particular portion of the space.

PERSPECTIVE DRAWING

Perspective drawing offers a natural view of interior space and for this reason is very popular for use in design presentations. Perspective sketching is also an excellent a design tool and is used as such by many designers throughout the design process. Many design students (and some design professionals) have difficulty creating clear, natural-looking perspective drawings. This is unfortunate, because perspective drawing can allow students and designers to explore and refine design ideas throughout the design process. Using perspective drawing only in finalized design presentations can result in weak design projects and lost opportunities for discovery.

An understanding of basic perspective principles allows designers to draw quickly and fairly accurately. Quick perspective drawings are helpful as visualization tools for designers. In addition, an understanding of basic principles and estimated sketching techniques allows for the creation of fresh, attractive drawings that can be used in design presentations.

The ability to draw simply measured or estimated freehand perspectives allows for the rapid expression of ideas, which helps in the generation of ideas and solutions. Certainly, the capacity to produce laboriously created mechanical perspective drawings is important in design practice, but equally important is the ability to express ideas rapidly.

PERSPECTIVE BASICS

Understanding the concept of the picture plane is fundamental to understanding perspective drawing. The PICTURE PLANE is an imaginary transparent plane through which the area to be drawn is viewed. The picture plane can be visualized as a giant sheet of glass standing between the viewer and the area to be drawn. Once the drawing is begun, the surface of the drawing paper represents this picture plane. We cannot create successful perspective drawings without first visualizing the picture plane and its relationship to the items to be drawn on the surface of the paper. Understanding that the paper surface can be seen as a reproduction of the picture plane is fundamental to good perspective drawing (Figure 3-5).

It is the relationship of an object to the picture plane (and to the location of the viewer) that creates a given perspective view of the object. For example, a box that has its front face (plane) parallel to the picture plane is in a position that creates a one point perspective drawing (Figure 3-6).

Turning the box so that the entire front corner is on edge in relation to the picture plane creates a two-point perspective view of the box (Figure 3-7).

Tweaking the box so that only the top (or bottom) corner touches the picture plane creates a three-point perspective view of the box (Figure 3-8).

All three types of perspective employ a HORIZON LINE representing the eye level of the viewer. A box held high above the viewer's eye level (horizon line) allows a view of the bottom of the box. As the box is moved below the eye level of the viewer (the horizon line), a view of the top of the box is possible. In all types of perspective drawing, perspective lines converge to a VANISHING POINT (or points, in two- and three-point perspectives).

The general location of the viewer is often called the STATION POINT. It is from this point in space that the item is seen by the view-

Figure 3-5
In perspective drawing the picture plane is an imaginary viewing plane that can be represented by the drawing surface.

Figure 3-6
A box drawn in one-point perspective has its front plane parallel to the picture plane.

Figure 3-7
A box drawn in two-point perspective has its front corner viewed on edge in relation to the picture plane.

Figure 3-8
All planes of the box are oblique to the picture plane when viewed in three-point perspective.
Drawings by Justin Thomson.

er. Another important perspective principle, shared by all three types of perspective, is the CONE OF VISION. The cone of vision represents the angle of view, or range of sight of the viewer. This concept is based on the reality that humans cannot view all of a space at a given time. As we approach a given space, we focus on one area at a time, owing to the natural limitations of our vision.

The cone of vision, or angle of view, can be seen as representing the natural limits of human sight. Elements that exist within the cone of vision of the viewer can generally be drawn without excessive distortion. Those elements that exist outside of the cone of vision become distorted and cannot be drawn successfully.

Perspective drawings show objects becoming smaller as they recede toward the vanishing point(s); that is, items decrease in size as they move away from the viewer. This perspective principle is referred to as DIMINUTION OF SIZE. As a result, a box drawn correctly will appear larger when closest to the viewer and smaller as it moves farther from the viewer. Because items diminish in size, they cannot be measured consistently in scale; therefore, a variety of methods of measurement have been devised.

Although there are a number of nuances that create more complicated relationships of object to picture plane and horizon line, those mentioned here are fundamental perspective relationships. An effective way to become skilled at drawing in perspective is to practice drawing simple boxes in various relationships to the picture plane and to the horizon line. The ability to sketch a box in perspective in such various relationships allows for the eventual capability to draw more complex objects constructed from boxlike forms. To sketch boxes in perspective successfully, additional information about perspective drawing is required.

ONE-POINT PERSPECTIVE

One-point perspective views portray an object or environment with one plane parallel to the picture plane. In addition to this parallel orientation to the picture plane, one-point perspective views make use of one vanishing point, located along the horizon line, to which all perspective lines converge. The horizon line is a horizontal line that represents the eye level of the viewer, usually between five and six feet from the floor. One-point perspective is considered the easiest type of perspective to draw, because the entire plane that is parallel to the picture plane can be measured in scale. Figure 3-9 illustrates one-point perspective principles.

Ease of construction of one-point perspective is also based on the fact that lines that are vertical in reality remain vertical, horizontal lines remain horizontal, and only lines indicating perspective depth are drawn converging to the vanishing point. Although they are easy to draw, one-point perspective views can be unnatural looking and can become distorted. Despite their drawbacks, one-point perspective drawings are highly useful during the early stages of design and are often used by designers for ideation (idea generation).

Two-Point Perspective

Two-point perspective drawings portray objects and volumes on edge in relationship to the picture plane. Another way of stating this is that two-point perspective depicts the primary faces of a volume oblique to the picture plane. This means that two-point perspectives offer a view of the front corner of objects or the rear corners of rooms and environments. In two-point perspective, an object's edge (or the corner of a room) is drawn first and can be used as a vertical measuring line from which perspective lines recede toward two vanishing points. The two vanishing points lie on the horizon line, one to the left and one to the right. As with one-point perspective drawings, the horizon line is always horizontal and represents the eye level of the viewer. Figure 3-10 illustrates the principles of two-point perspective.

Apart from the horizon line and elements that lie along the horizon line, there are no horizontal lines found in accurate two-point perspective drawings. Instead, lines that are not true verticals converge to one of the two vanishing points. Only one vertical measuring line can be drawn in scale owing to the fact that perspective lines converge to two vanishing points, causing objects to look smaller as they recede away from the viewer toward the vanishing points. Two-point perspective drawings can be tricky to measure and can be confusing to create. However, two-point perspective drawings appear more natural and suffer from less distortion than other types of perspective.

Three-Point Perspective

Three-point perspective is not commonly used in traditional illustration of interior space. Three-point perspective portrays an object or volume with all principle faces oblique to the picture plane. All lines in this type of perspective converge to vanishing points. Generally, three-point perspectives are constructed with two vanishing points on the horizon line, one to the left and one to the right, with an additional vanishing point above or below the horizon line. It is best to center the third vanishing point above or below the left and right vanishing point. Figure 3-11 is a quick reference to three-point perspective principles.

The use of three vanishing points creates highly dynamic drawings that may easily become distorted. Because all lines converge to vanishing points, no true scale measuring line can be employed. This means that drawing three-point perspectives requires good visualization skills. Three-point perspective is most useful for portraying in drawings single objects, such as furniture or products, that by design should be dynamic, unusual, or attention grabbing. Three-point perspective creates an "ant 's eye view" or "bird 's eye view" and is also used in some types of animation.

Developing Visual Skills

In order to develop visual skills and learn to "see" in perspective, students should practice drawing simple "square-looking" boxes in one-, two- and three-point perspective. I believe that the ability to draw accurate-looking boxes lies at the heart of successful perspective drawing. Figure 3-12 illustrates important principles of perspective sketching.

Boxes drawn in two-point perspective will appear distorted when the two vanishing points are located too close to each other on the horizon line. The vanishing points should be kept far enough apart to create an angle of 90 DEGREES or greater at the front edge of the cube. At the same time, the front edge of the cube should be less than 140 DEGREES (see Figure 3-12).

In two-point perspective the front corner (also known as the vertical leading edge) of an object is often used as a VERTICAL MEASURING LINE. This vertical measuring line can be scaled and then used to measure portions of the object that recede toward the vanishing points. Vertical measuring lines allow for fairly accurate measurement of vertical elements of drawings. In principle, this vertical measuring line is the only element of a drawing that can be accurately scaled, because the front corner that serves as a measuring line is touching the picture plane—or is very close to it (see Figure 3-12).

For dimensions that cannot be measured on vertical surfaces, a number of very simple proportional devices can be employed. One such method of proportional perspective measurement involves the use of DIAGONAL LINES as a means of subdividing squares and rectangular planes in perspective. Each face of a square can be subdivided into visually equal portions at the intersection of two diagonals. The intersection of diagonals drawn from corner to corner of a square locates the midpoint of that square. Rectangular planes are also divided in this manner. Diagonal subdivision of rectangular planes is a significant perspective principle and is useful in all methods of perspective drawing (see Figure 3-12).

The use of diagonals can also aid in adding, extending, and duplicating boxes drawn in perspective. One method of doing this requires locating the midpoint of a single box or cube, then drawing a diagonal from the bottom corner of the cube through the midpoint of the far side of the cube. The diagonal is then extended from the midpoint to the top perspective line (that which recedes to the vanishing point). Where the diagonal meets the perspective line of the original cube, a new vertical is drawn, creating a second square that is visually equal in perspective (see Figure 3-12).

It is useful to learn to draw boxes with elements that have slanted surfaces, such as gabled roofs. These slanted surfaces do not fall on the primary horizon line. Instead, the lines that form the slanting surfaces converge at a point directly above or below the vanishing point for the box. This point, known as a "VANISHING TRACE" (after Ching, 1975), is a line to which all parallel lines in the same plane will converge. A vanishing trace is employed because lines that are parallel always converge at a common point (see Figure 3-12).

A vanishing trace is also useful in relation to drawing stairs. Stairs can be drawn by first plotting the base of the stair (the width and depth as found on the floor plane). The height of the stair must then be locat-

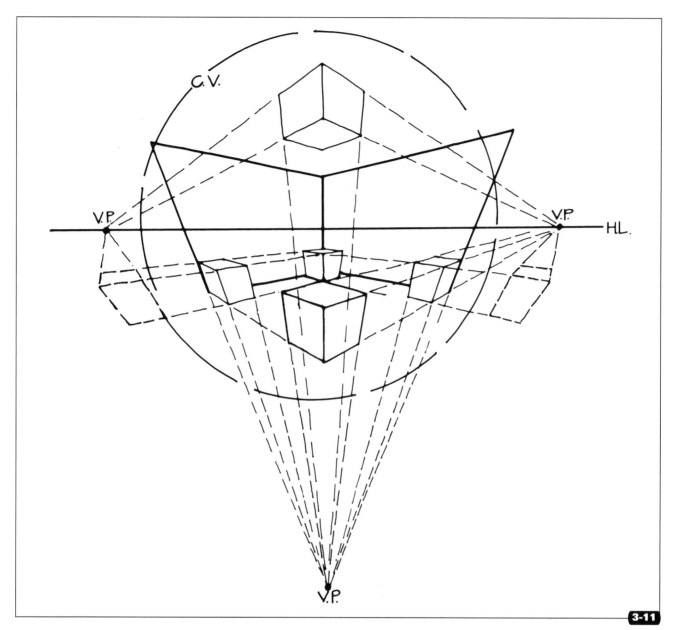

Figure 3-9

Quick reference: one-point perspective principles.

Perspective lines converge to a single vanishing point (V. P.), located on the horizon line (H.L.). The front faces of the cubes and the back wall of a room are viewed parallel to the picture plane. Those elements with faces touching the picture plane can be drawn in scale. One-point perspective drawings have true vertical, horizontal, and perspective (depth) lines. Items located outside of the cone of vision (C.V.) tend to appear distorted

Figure 3-10

Quick reference: two-point perspective principles.

Perspective lines converge to two vanishing points (V. P.s), located on the horizon line (H.L.). Boxes are viewed from the front corner, and rooms generally from the back corner in relation to the picture plane. Two-point perspective drawings have true vertical lines as well as perspective (depth) lines. In two point perspective, the front edge (or back edge) touching the picture plane can be measured in scale. Items located outside of the cone of vision (C.V.) tend to appear distorted. As with all forms of perspective, items appear to diminish in size as they recede from viewer.

Figure 3-11

Quick reference: three-point perspective principles.

Perspective lines converge to three vanishing points (V. P.s), two located on the horizon line (H.L.) and one usually above or below the horizon line. All planes of a box are oblique to the picture plane. All lines drawn in three-point perspective drawings converge to a vanishing point. No portion of a three-point perspective drawing can be measured in scale. Items located outside the cone of vision (C.V.) tend to appear distorted. As with all forms of perspective, items appear to diminish in size as they recede from viewer.

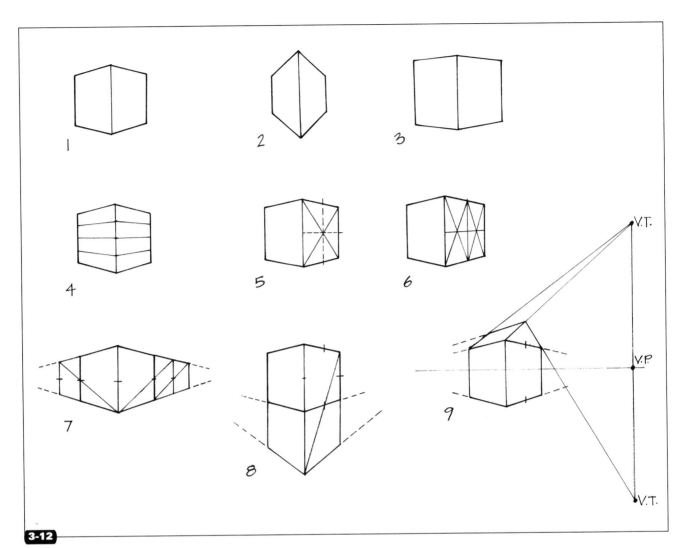

Figure 3-12

Quick reference: sketching in two-point perspective.

1. Practice drawing boxes that look square.
2. Boxes look distorted when the front corner equals less than 90 degrees.
3. Boxes look distorted when the front corner equals greater than 140 degrees.
4. The front corner can be divided equally to serve as a measuring line.
5. Bisecting diagonals divide a square drawn in perspective.
6. Diagonals also divide rectangles.
7. Boxes can be extended using diagonals. Extend a diagonal from bottom corner through midpoint of a square. Where the diagonal meets the perspective line (line to V.P.), a new box is formed.
8. Diagonals can also extend a box vertically.
9. Slanting parallel lines converge at a common point. This point is called a vanishing trace (after Ching, 1975), or V.T., and is directly below or above the V.P.

ed on a height plane. The height plane must be divided equally (use the forward vertical as a measuring line) in increments that equal the required number of risers. The first riser can be found by drawing a line from the appropriate vanishing point forward through the noted riser height and onward to the riser location as noted on the floor plane.

The next step involves drawing the vanishing trace. A vanishing trace is found by drawing a diagonal line from the forward location of the height of the riser to the top of the stair run (as measured on the height plane) and onward to a location directly above the vanishing point. With this vanishing trace located, a second diagonal is drawn to the opposite side of the stair. Risers and treads are then located where measuring increments brought forward from vanishing points intersect with diagonals. Figure 3-13 gives instructions for stair construction.

Circles and curves are drawn as ELLIPSES in perspective. An understanding of ellipses and how they are drawn can help create perspective drawings that are natural looking (Figures 3-14 and 3-15).

Understanding the relationship of the major and minor axes of an ellipse is essential to successful perspective drawing. The MAJOR

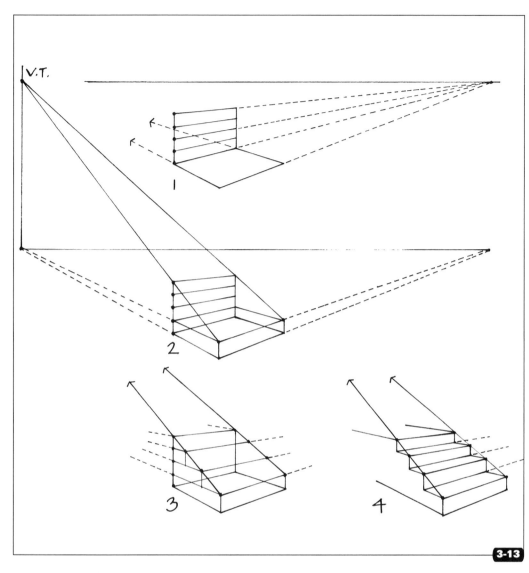

Figure 3-13
Sketching stairs in two-point
perspective.

1. By measurement or
   estimation, plot the width
   and depth of the stairs on
   the floor plan. Locate a
   height plane by extending
   vertical lines to the
   appropriate height (the top
   of the stair run). Divide the
   height plane to create the
   appropriate
   number of risers.

2. Draw a line from the
   vanishing point through the
   height plane at the first riser
   measurement this creates
   the first riser. Draw a
   diagonal line from the
   forward height of the first
   riser through the top of the
   height plane and continue
   this diagonal until it is
   directly above the V.P. this is
   the vanishing trace (V.T.)
   Draw a second diagonal
   from the vanishing trace to
   the location opposite the
   forward riser.

3. Draw lines from the V.P.
   through each riser
   measurement on the height
   plane. Continue these lines
   until they intersect with
   diagonals these are the
   forward riser locations.

4. Tread locations are found by
   extending vertical lines
   down to the next riser
   measurement; lines
   indicating treads converge to
   the appropriate vanishing
   point.

AXIS is an imaginary line that is found at the widest part of an ellipse, and the MINOR AXIS is found at the narrow diameter of the ellipse. An ellipse's major axis is greater than its minor axis. The major and minor axes always appear at right angles (90 degrees) to each other regardless of the position of the object. When found on horizontal planes, such as floors and ceilings, an ellipse 's major axis is always horizontal.

The centerline of a cylinder or cylindrical object is drawn as an extension of the minor axis. Because it is an extension of the minor axis, this centerline always appears at a right angle to the major axis. This means that the centerline of a complicated object, such as the axle of a wheel or the cylindrical base of a piece of furniture, can be drawn as an extension of the minor axis.

Understanding the relationship of the minor and major axes and the location of the centerline can eliminate distortion in the drawing of circular forms in perspective, allowing for freehand sketching of ellipses as well as construction of complex linear perspectives.

One method of ellipse construction involves using squares as an approximation guide for the ellipse (Figure 3-15). This is done by

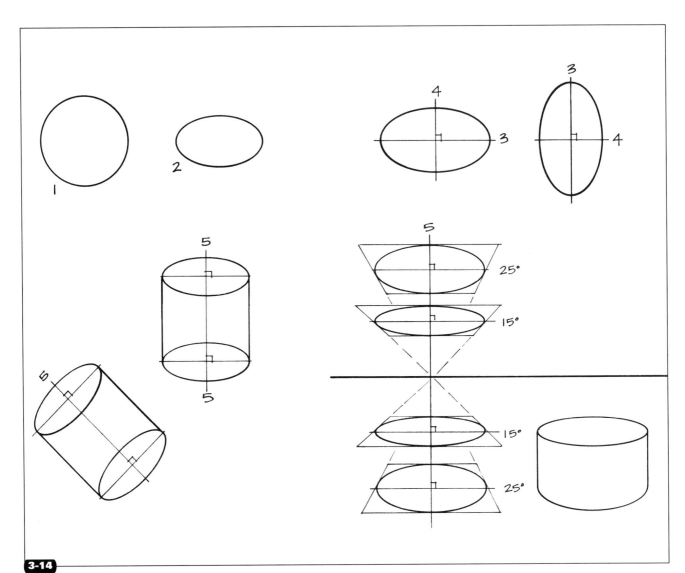

3-14

Figure 3-14

Ellipses

1. Circle.

2. Ellipse. In perspective drawings, circles are drawn as ellipses.

3. The major axis is found at the widest diameter of an ellipse.

4. The minor axis is found at the narrow diameter, and is always at 90 degrees to the major axis.

5. The centerline of a cylinder is drawn as an extension of the minor axis (also at 90 degrees to major axis).

6. When found on a horizontal plane such as a floor, the major axis is horizontal. Our view of the ellipse varies according to the location of our eye level (horizon line); elliptical templates are used to easily approximate the various views.

first drawing a square in perspective, then dividing the square using a diagonal. On each diagonal, approximately two-thirds distance from the center point of the square, a dot (or mark) is drawn. The ellipse is then approximated by drawing curved lines from the dots on the diagonals to the midpoints of each side of the square. With the rough approximation complete, the major and minor axes can be approximated to aid in refinement. The minor and major axes should not be confused with the diagonal divisions of the square, as these are separate items.

Many designers use elliptical templates to create accurate ellipses and curvilinear forms. The use of elliptical templates is based on the locations of the major axis, the minor axis, and the centerline of the form.

The square-looking box drawn accurately in perspective is the single most effective tool in simple freehand drawing. It is worthwhile for students to practice by filling pages with boxes drawn to look square in two-point perspective. Once this skill has been developed, the box is drawn as an enclosing form, like a packing crate, then portions of the

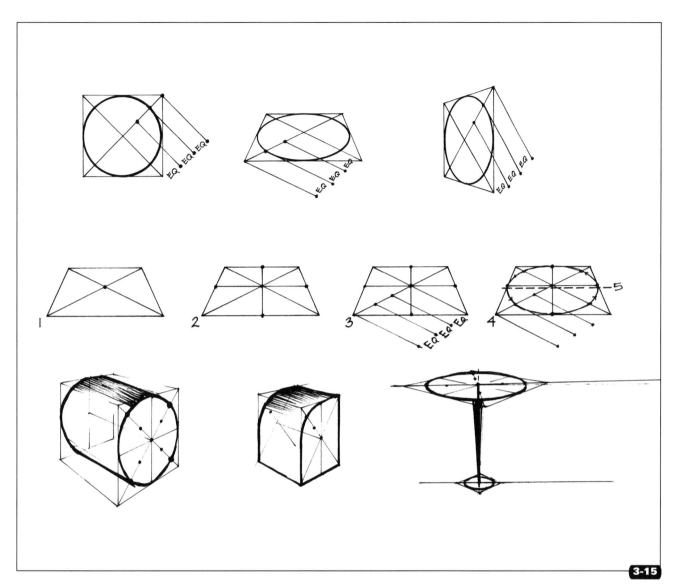

Figure 3-15
Quick reference: ellipse construction.

Ellipses can be estimated by creating an enclosing square and plotting locations on diagonals:

1. Create an enclosing square, divide the square with diagonals (as in diagonal division). Mark the center of the square as located by the diagonals.

2. From the center of the square, extend lines vertically and horizontally; these lines will define midpoints of the enclosing square. Mark the locations where these lines are tangent to (touching) the enclosing square.

3. Divide each quarter of the diagonal into thirds and make marks at these locations.

4. Sketch the ellipse by locating the mark two thirds from center and drawing connecting curvilinear lines from the two thirds mark to the adjacent midpoint mark. Refine the ellipse by visual assessment.

5. Note: quarter divisions of the square are not the major and minor axes. These divisions are for estimation purposes only. The major axis is actually slightly forward of center (dashed line).

Figure 3-16
Quick reference: two-point sketching using estimated boxes.

1. Sketch a box that "looks square." Make sure the vanishing points are generously spaced. Create a measuring line at the front corner of the box. Mark equal divisions of the measuring line (these can be eyeballed or estimated with diagonal division).

2. Use the measuring line and diagonal division to rough out details and proportions.
3. Overlay with clean tracing paper and refine details.
4. Use a clean overlay for a final drawing; a combination of freehand and drafted lines often look best.
Drawing by Leanne Larson.

3-16

REFERENCES

Ching, Frank. *Architectural Graphics*. New York: John Wiley & Sons, 1996.

Ching, Frank. *A Visual Dictionary of Architecture*. New York: John Wiley & Sons, 1995.

Drpic, Ivo. *Sketching and Rendering Interior Space*. New York: Whitney Library of Design, 1988.

Forseth, Kevin, and David Vaughn. *Graphics for Architecture*. New York: John Wiley & Sons, 1980.

Hanks, Kurt, and Larry Belliston. *Rapid Viz*. Los Altos, CA: William Kaufman, 1980.

McGarry, Richard, and Greg Madsen. *Marker Magic: The Rendering Problem Solver for Designers*. New York: Van Nostrand Reinhold, 1993.

Pile, John. *Perspective for Interior Designers*. New York: Whitney Library of Design, 1985.

Porter, Tom. *Architectural Drawing*. New York: Van Nostrand Reinhold, 1990.

box are subtracted to reveal the object within (Figure 3-16). Starting with a simple box, and adding boxes using diagonal division, allows us to sketch items in boxes that are not square but may be elongated in a number of directions.

Subtracting and adding approximated elliptical elements allows us to create complex objects. The ability to visually assess freehand perspective drawings that have been constructed from simple boxes lets us understand and see form and spatial relationships. Employing the principles of perspective mentioned thus far allows for better drawing and for the use of perspective drawing as a design tool.

Drawing and Sketching Interior Environments

ESTIMATED ONE-POINT INTERIOR PERSPECTIVE DRAWINGS

The same concepts that allow us to sketch objects using enclosing boxes can be employed in sketching interior environments. There are many methods of measured, linear perspective drawing that work well in the creation of accurate, beautiful drawings. However, it is important to note that all of the most accurate and refined methods of perspective drawing require a great deal of time ranging from one to eight hours. These may be appropriate for final design development presentations, but time constraints require designers to develop quick sketching techniques in order to use drawings throughout the design process. Quick sketching is beneficial as a design tool, a presentation tool, and a way of seeing the world and recording details successfully.

The easiest method of quick sketching interior environments has as its foundation the box sketching techniques discussed previously. This estimated method allows us to create a perspective of a ten-foot-square room by drawing a giant ten-foot-square box in one-point perspective. Figure 4-1 is a quick reference to this estimated one-point perspective method. It is important to note that this method is unusual in that it requires that a square-looking room is estimated, necessitating visual accuracy developed by practice.

The estimated sketch method is started by drawing a horizontal line to serve as a the horizon line; this is the eye level of the viewer. A square (that serves as the back wall of the room) can then be drawn that is ten feet by ten feet (in any appropriate scale or eyeballed). The horizon line should bisect the square at its vertical midpoint. Next, a single vanishing point is located on the horizon line slightly left or right of center. Perspective lines indicating depth are created by drawing lines from the vanishing point through all four corners of the square. The overall depth of the room is simply estimated.

The key to this method is the ability to estimate the forward depth of the square room. The depth must be estimated in a way that makes the room "look square." This is the tricky part—which takes some practice. Once this is accomplished, architectural elements can be drawn by using measurements found on the back wall (the original square) and estimating depth. Diagonal bisection of planes can be used to find depths of walls and corresponding objects.

Because many rooms do not have ten-foot ceilings, it is often necessary to "lower" the ceiling by redrawing it at eight to nine feet. This is accomplished by locating the desired height on the back wall (the original measured square) and cutting the wall off at the desired height. imilarly, ceilings can be raised by adding the appropriate dimension to the back wall (the original square) and extending the walls to the desired height.

Figure 4-1

Quick reference: estimated one-point interior sketching.

1. Draw a 10′ x 10′ square in a workable scale (1/2-inch or 1-inch).
2. Divide the square using diagonals. Draw a horizontal line through the center this is the horizon line (H.L.); it is at roughly 5′ high. Place a vanishing point on the horizon line slightly left or right of center.
3. Draw perspective lines from the V.P. thorough the corners of the original square, creating wall and ceiling lines. Now estimate the depth of the room—make it look square.
4. Use diagonals to divide the original square (see Figure 3-12), which is now the back wall. By dividing the back equally in four, you will create 30′ height increments.
5. If necessary, a grid can be estimated through diagonal division. On side walls, verticals are located where height lines intersect diagonals.
6. Use measuring increments (created in step 4) or a grid to locate objects and architectural elements.
7. Use a clean overlay to create a line drawing.
8. To raise or lower the ceiling, simply draw lines from the V.P. to the appropriate height on the back wall and extend these lines forward. Diagonal extensions can be used to enlarge the room (see Figure 3-12). Curves are found by plotting and sketching in appropriate locations.

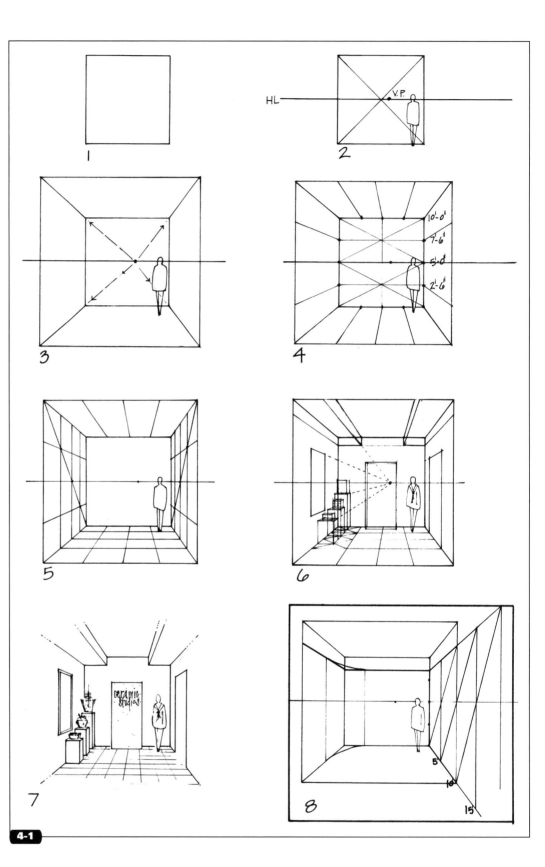

4-1

Most rooms are not perfectly square, and this method allows for the original ten-by-ten square to serve as the starting point for a room of another shape. Dividing and adding to the room, using diagonal bisection, allows for the creation of a variety of room sizes. Once again, the ability to see and create the original square room and use it as a guide for drawing a more complicated environment is the key to the success of this method.

In drawing estimated one-point interior perspectives, complicated items or architectural elements are easiest to draw when placed on the wall(s) parallel to the picture plane. The location of the single vanishing point is important, because walls and objects located very close to their vanishing points can become quite distorted. It is useful to draw a few quick thumbnail sketches of the space, using the estimation method, to locate the vanishing point and visualize the space being drawn. Thumbnail sketches aid in the location of an appropriate view of the space and the location of the vanishing point.

The estimated method is an approximation method. Measurements are based on rough approximations. For example, the horizon line is placed at roughly five feet in height, providing a view of the space from a five-foot eye level. We can imagine that most pieces of furniture fit into a thirty-inch-high packing crate. Therefore, much of the furniture is roughed in as thirty-inch-high boxes. Human figures drawn to scale should be included in interior perspectives and are best placed with eye levels at (or near) the horizon line. More information regarding scale figures can be found in Appendix 2.

This method of quick sketching, using rough approximations, allows designers to draw space as they design it. It also allows perspective drawing to be integrated into the design process during the schematic design and design development phases of a project (Figure 4-2). The estimation method can be used to draw one-point perspectives from above (Figure 4-3). Most of the more refined methods of linear perspective require complete scaled plans and elevations, thus necessitating that the design be complete prior to the creation of the perspective drawings. The more refined perspectives are most useful means of presentation but are not as helpful as a quick means of exploring design options or brainstorming.

ESTIMATED TWO-POINT INTERIOR PERSPECTIVE DRAWINGS

One-point interiors are helpful and very easy to create but are limited in use because of problems with distortion, particularly in drawing furniture and free standing objects. Because of the limitations of one-point perspective, it is important to learn to draw two-point interior perspectives quickly, using the estimation method.

Figure 4-2
Example of estimated one-point
interior perspective drawing.
Drawing by Ardella Pieper.

The same concepts used in drawing boxes and estimated one-point interiors are employed in estimated two-point perspective sketching. In the two-point method a ten-by-ten square room is drawn first as a guideline for further development. Figure 4-4 is a quick reference for the estimated two-point perspective method.

The ten-by-ten room is created by first drawing a single vertical measuring line with four equal segments noted (in any appropriate scale or eyeballed). This vertical measuring line serves two important functions: first, it is the only true measuring device in the drawing; and, second, it can become the back corner of the room(s) being drawn. A horizontal line is then drawn through the middle of the vertical line (bisecting it at the five-foot mark). This is the horizon line or viewer's eye level.

Two vanishing points must be placed on the horizon line. One should be located fairly close to the vertical measuring line; this is referred to as the near vanishing point. The second should be locat-

4-3

ed far from the vertical measuring line; this is referred to as the far vanishing point.

Next, draw a line from the near vanishing point to the very bottom of the vertical measuring line and extend it forward, creating the floor line. Repeat the process with the far vanishing point. Lines are then drawn from each vanishing point to the very top (the tenth increment) of the vertical measuring line and extended forward, creating the ceiling line.

At this point in the drawing we have created the floor, two walls, and the ceiling location of the room. The depth of the room must now be estimated. The overall room depth is approximated by visually assessing the room and creating a square-looking box of a room. As with one-point estimation, this is the tricky part. The key is the ability to *estimate* the depth of a square ten-by-ten room, which takes some practice.

With the use of this method, architectural elements and freestanding objects are located by measurement and estimation. The vertical measuring line can be used to find vertical measurements; these are taken from the vanishing point through the vertical measuring line and plotted on the appropriate wall. In cases where objects are freestanding, heights can be determined by extending a line from the vanishing point through the appropriate height on the wall to the location of the object. Depths are estimated using diagonal division and extension. This is done by dividing the walls with diagonals; the midpoint of the room is found at the intersection of the two diagonals.

The originally estimated square room can be modified to create a lower or higher ceiling by simply extending or reducing the dimensions of the original vertical measuring line and extending lines to the vanishing points. The walls of the room can easily be reconfigured by diagonal subdivision and extension. The ability to see and create the

Figure 4-3
Estimated one-point sketch used for view from above.

Figure 4-4

Quick reference: estimated two-point interior sketching.

1. Draw a single vertical line to serve as a measuring line. Divide the line into four equal segments. At the midpoint, draw a horizontal line; this is the horizon line (H.L.).

2. Place two vanishing points on the H.L., one near to (N.V.P.) and one far from (F.V.P.) the measuring line. Draw lines from each V.P. through the top and bottom of the measuring line. This creates floor and ceiling lines. Now estimate the depth of room—make it look square.

3. Draw lines from each V.P. through all increments on the measuring line; these will serve as height measurement lines.

4. To create a grid, draw diagonals on each wall. Then, at the intersection of the diagonal and each height line, draw a vertical.

5. Use the grid to estimate architectural elements and objects. Note: grids are not always necessary; for simple spaces it is best to simply estimate measurements.

6. Use a clean overlay for tracing and refining the drawing.

7. Raise or lower the ceiling by estimating the desired height. Extend the room using diagonal division (see Figure 3-12).

8. Curved surfaces are estimated by using a grid.

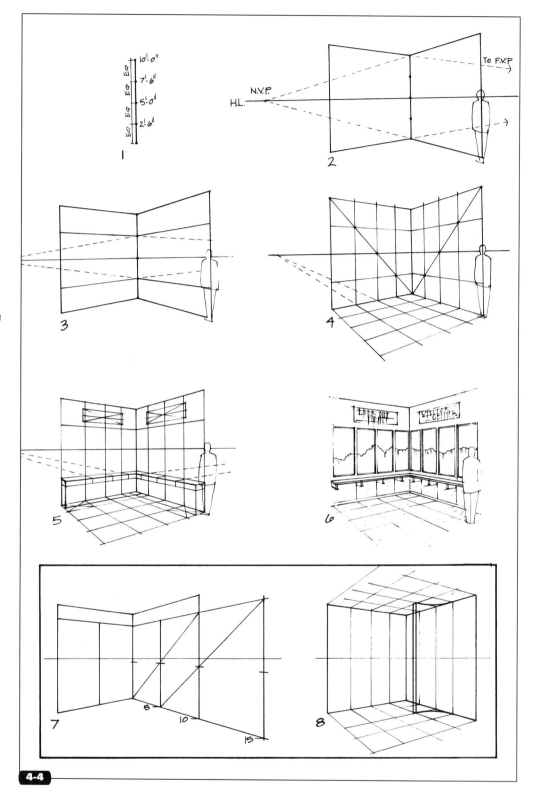

4-4

original square-looking room and use it as a guide for drawing a more complicated environment is the key to the success of this method.

In drawing two-point interior perspectives, complicated items and architectural elements are easiest to draw when placed on the wall created by the far vanishing point. This is because the wall generated by the near vanishing point tends to become distorted. A common distortion problem in two-point perspective drawing is caused by locating the two vanishing points too close to each other. This creates a distorted, unnatural-looking view of the space. If in the process of using this method your drawing becomes distorted, it is best to start over with the vanishing points located farther from each other.

As with one-point sketches, it is useful to do a few thumbnail sketches of the space, to locate the vanishing points, and visualize the space being drawn. Thumbnail sketches allow for the location of an appropriate view of the space and the proper positioning of the vanishing points.

The estimated two-point perspective method is an approximation method. Measurements are based on rough approximations. For example, the horizon line is placed at roughly five feet in height. This gives the drawing the overall view at a five-foot eye level of the viewer. We can imagine that most pieces of furniture fit into a thirty-inch-high packing crate. Therefore, much of the furniture can be sketched into the space as thirty-inch-high boxes. Human figures drawn to scale should be included in interior perspectives and are best placed with eye levels located at or near the horizon line. More information about scale figures may be found in Appendix 2.

Methods of estimated sketching, using rough approximation as described here (also known as "eyeballing" drawings), permit designers to draw a space as they design it. This type of sketching allows perspective drawing to be integrated into the design process. Sketching in perspective lets us visualize spaces three-dimensionally rather than merely view space in plan, where a sense of volume is often missing. Visualization skills are fundamental to the design of interior environments.

Most of the more refined methods of linear perspective require complete scaled plans and elevations, thus necessitating the design to be complete prior to the creation of the perspective drawings. The more refined perspectives often appear highly realistic in contrast to the estimated methods. Refined, measured linear perspectives are most useful as a means of presentation for clients, end users, real estate professionals, investors, and the general public.

REFINED LINEAR PERSPECTIVE METHODS

The perspective drawing concepts and skills covered thus far can help us gain valuable visualization skills. These skills are easily transferred to the refined, measured methods of linear perspective. Therefore, the ability to draw well in estimated perspective allows us to draw well in refined, precisely measured perspectives.

The ability to create refined perspective presentation drawings is useful for all environmental designers. Most firms have at least one employee (and often several) who is considered to be a perspective drawing or rendering specialist. Such individuals are often called upon to do much of the detailed perspective drawing and rendering for the firm. It is also quite common for firms to hire professional design illustrators and renderers to create highly detailed drawings as required for particular project presentations. Firms often select a particular professional illustrator's style to enhance a particular project. This points to the fact that there is never a single way to illustrate space; instead, there are a range of stylistic approaches.

A wide variety of methods of measured perspective drawing are used in practice. I have found that certain methods work best for certain people. People who draw well in measured perspective employ the particular method that works best for them. For this reason a variety of methods are briefly discussed and illustrated in the following sections. Students should experiment with the methods described to discover a personal method of measured perspective drawing.

Two-Point Plan Projection Method

Two-point plan projection is also known as the "common method" or the "office method." This is a method used by students and professionals alike. A comparable method is commonly used for exterior perspectives, and a similar one-point method is used as well. The plan projection method requires a completed, scaled floor plan and scaled elevations. Figures 4-5a and 4-5b illustrate step-by-step plan projection instructions.

This method is completely different from any perspective methods discussed previously. Although it is useful and highly accurate, it can be confusing at first because it requires going back and forth from plan view to perspective view. To minimize confusion, one must understand that the floor plan is used to "set up" the final perspective elements and measurements. In this method the floor plan is manipulated to provide information that is projected onto the perspective drawing.

To begin this method, decisions must be made in regard to what view of the space is desired, the location of the viewer, and the cone of vision. Key elements of the space must be included within a 60-degree cone of vision. With decisions made regarding the areas to be shown and the orientation of the viewer, the plan is "set up" against the picture plane (also drawn in plan).

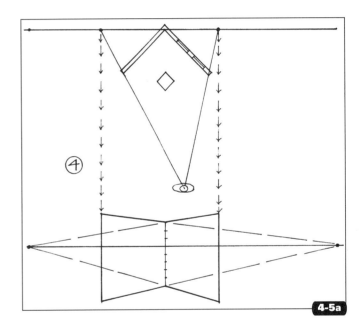

4-5a

Figure 4-5a

Quick reference: two-point plan projection.

1. Draw a horizontal line this is the picture plane (P.P.). Select the desired angle of view and orient the plan so that the rear corner touches the picture plane. Locate the station point (S.P.); make sure all desired elements fit within a 60 degree cone of vision projecting from the S.P. to the desired areas in plan. Locate the station point one to three times the height of the interior space from the focal point of the drawing.

2. Draw lines from the S.P. to the P.P. that are parallel to the walls of the floor plan; the locations of the intersections of these lines and the P.P. are the set up vanishing points, vanishing point right (V.P.R) and vanishing point left (V.P.L).

3. Draw a horizontal line below the plan setup; this is the horizon line (H.L.). Project the location of V.P.L. and V.P.R vertically to the H.L.

this relocates the vanishing points. Project a line from the rear corner of plan vertically to the H.L this will be the measuring line (M.L.). It can be measured in scale (to match plan); it will also be the back corner of the room. The horizon line must be located at 5' to 6' in scale on the M.L. (normal eye

level).

4. Draw lines from the V.P.L. through the top and bottom of the M.L. these are the wall and floor lines. Repeat this step with V.P.R. Next, draw lines from the S.P. through the ends of walls (in plan) to the P.P. Project these locations vertically onto the drawing.

Figure 4-5a

5. Draw lines from the S.P. through window locations, or any other elements (on plan), to the P.P. Project these locations vertically onto the drawing. Heights are determined by measuring from M.L. or from an available elevation.

Hint: Often when a drawing looks wrong or "off," it is because a location was not projected from the P.P.

4-5a

The plan setup must also include the location of the viewer in plan; this is known as the station point, but I like my students to think of it as the head of the viewer in plan. The station point, or location of the viewer, is an extremely important component to the success of this method. The location of the station point dictates the view of the space, as well as the cone of vision and other key elements such as the location of the vanishing points.

With the plan set up against the picture plane and the station point located, the vanishing points can be located on the picture plane in plan. This is done by drawing lines from the station point parallel to the walls of the room (or building) that terminate at the picture plane. " This method requires that lines be drawn from the station point to the location on the plan, to the picture plane, and then projected onto the perspective drawing.

Most students find it helpful to recognize two separate types of activities within this method: (1) those set up in plan and related to the picture plane and (2) those then projected from the picture plane to the perspective drawing. Measurements of width and depth are projected from the picture plane onto the perspective drawings. Heights are measured from the measuring line and tranferred as needed or taken from an elevation.

The plan projection method is generally accurate and provides an excellent perspective framework. The method can be time-consuming and sometimes leads to unexpected distortion, requiring the entire process to be completed a second time. I find that the method works best for environments based on simple geometric forms rather than those based on complex or organic forms.

P.P.

① ⊙ S.P.

② a
b
c ⊙ S.P.

◇

◇

③ M.L
V.P.L. V.P.R.
c

④

Figure 4-5b
Quick reference: locating
freestanding objects using plan projection.

1. Draw lines form the S.P. through
   the edges of the object and
   extend them to the P.P. Project
   these locations vertically onto
   the drawing.
2. To find a floor location, first
   transfer the furniture location
   onto walls in plan setup (a).
   Then draw lines from the S.P.
   to locations on walls; extend
   the lines to P.P. Next project
   locations on the P.P. vertically
   to the appropriate wall in the
   drawing (b). Draw a line from
   the V.P. to the location where
   lthe wall projection meets the
   floor (c); extend these lines
   forward onto the object to find
   the floor location.
3. Find the height of objects by
   drawing a line from V.P. (in this
   case, V.P.R.) through the
   appropriate height on the M.L.
   to the wall location (c).
4. The object is completed
   with lines drawn to the
   appropriate vanishing points.

   Hint: Often when a drawing
   looks wrong or "off," it is because
   a location was not
   projected from the P.P.

4-5b

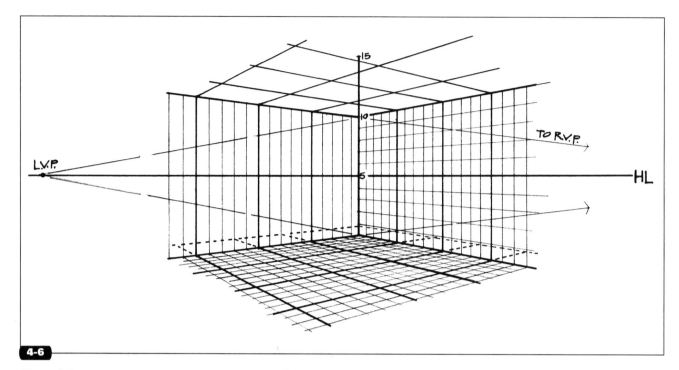

Figure 4-6
A prepared perspective grid chart.

PREPARED PERSPECTIVE GRID CHARTS

Prepared perspective charts are used by many designers and design illustrators. Charts are popular owing to their ease of use and speed of construction. Many designers and illustrators use only prepared charts in the construction of perspective drawings.

The charts provide a perspective framework including horizon line, location of viewer, cone of vision, vanishing points, and measuring devices. This framework allows items to be located, measured, and drawn to appropriate vanishing points. Visual accuracy and the ability to draw ellipses and square-looking boxes are required in the use of prepared charts, just as they are in quick sketching. These skills are necessary because grids merely provide a perspective framework and measuring system—they do not do the drawing for you.

Perspective charts are based on a set of given conditions. The location and height of viewer (and corresponding horizon line), vanishing points, cone of vision, measuring increments, and the overall visual emphasis of the space are all given within a particular chart. For this reason it is helpful to keep a set of charts with varying views and spatial relationships for use in various projects. Generally, perspective charts cover a huge area and must be manipulated and measured to define the space required in a drawing.

Because the charts contain hundreds of lines, they can be confusing and difficult to "read." It is a good idea to use a variety of colored pencils on tracing paper overlays to define the space and record important elements. Elements that establish the space, such as the horizon line, vanishing points, vertical measuring lines, and wall,

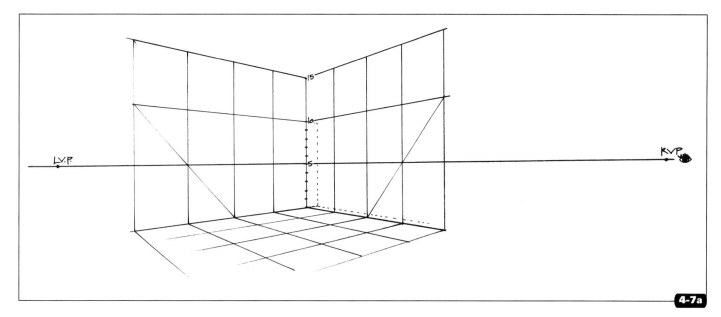

Figure 4-7a
The prepared chart customized for a particular project, the Royal Pavilion, Brighton, England.
Drawing by Leanne Larson.

floor, and ceiling grid lines, can be transferred to tracing paper using various colors. With these elements and other useful notes recorded, the original grid can be removed and a customized grid is created. The customized grid should be overlaid with tracing paper and kept for future reference.

Grid charts are useful, relatively quick, very accurate, and adaptable. Because one chart will not work for all projects, a series of charts is worth having. And, as discussed, all projects require that the grid be manipulated or customized to some degree, and this can be confusing, especially for beginners. Figure 4-6 is an example of a prepared grid. Figures 4-7a to 4-7h are a sequence of drawings using a prepared grid (see figures C-21a and C-21b for color renderings of this drawing). See figures C-22a and C-22b for drawings based on a grid used by a professional illustrator.

PERSPECTIVES TRACED
FROM PHOTOGRAPHS

Photographs can be traced to form a perspective framework. This method is especially useful in renovation of existing space where a photograph of existing conditions is used. This method works best if a photograph can be taken from the desired vantage point. In this situation it is necessary to be careful that the photograph is clearly taken from a one-point or two-point perspective vantage point. Once the photograph is processed, it can be enlarged, if necessary, on a photocopying machine. The enlargement is then overlaid with tracing paper, and the drawing can be constructed. Figure 4-8 is a quick reference of this method.

If the photograph is taken with the primary wall parallel to the camera lens (picture plane), a one-point perspective view is generated.

4-7b

4-7e

4-7c

4-7f

4-7d

4-7g

Figures 4-7b to 4-7h
The sequence of drawings prepared with the use of a grid, leading to a final line drawing the Royal Pavilion, Brighton, England (see Figure C-20b for a color rendering of this drawing). Drawings by Leanne Larson.

4-7h

The drawing in this case is constructed with one vanishing point located on the horizon line. This is done by tracing over the lines that form the floor and ceiling lines (or any series of major perspective lines). Where these lines converge is the vanishing point.

A horizontal line is drawn through the vanishing point, and this serves as the horizon line. It is useful to check this location by tracing perspective lines from an additional object in the space and making sure they converge at the same vanishing point. With the vanishing point and horizon line noted, new or proposed design elements can be "sketched into" the space. Items to be retained in the proposed design can simply be traced from the photograph. Figure 4-8 illustrates this process.

Two-point perspectives can be drawn from photographs that show the two main walls or elements as oblique to the camera lens (picture plane). The system is similar to that used in one-point tracing, except for the fact that two vanishing points must be located and placed on the horizon line. Most often, the correct vanishing point can be located by tracing the left floor and ceiling lines (or the corresponding lines of some significant object) to a point of convergence. The left vanishing point is estimated by tracing the right

Figure 4-8
Quick reference: tracing from photographs.

1. This photograph sets up a one-point view of the interior, because the back wall is parallel to the picture plane (camera lens). Trace over the lines that form the walls and ceiling; these will lead to a single vanishing point. Draw a horizontal line through the vanishing point; this is the horizon line.
2. New or proposed items are drawn using the vanishing point and the horizon line.
3. Trace items that will be retained from the photographic image. Add entourage elements such as plants, figures, or fixtures.

floor and ceiling lines (or the corresponding lines of some significant object) to a point of convergence.

A horizon line is created by drawing a horizontal line connecting the right and left vanishing points. It is imperative that the horizon line link the two vanishing points with a single horizontal line. With the two vanishing points and horizon line located, proposed changes can be sketched into the drawing. All elements to be retained in the proposed design may be traced into the drawing.

Generally, photographs taken of existing spaces include a number of interesting background and foreground elements. Human figures, plants, and details of daily life are often captured in photographs. These elements can be traced into the drawing to add interest and liveliness. Students often remove these items and, in so doing, create lifeless drawings.

Photographic slides or transparencies also may be traced to create a perspective framework system. This is done by projecting a slide onto a screen or wall and following the same procedures described for photographic tracing.

Students are sometimes reluctant to trace perspective drawings from photographic images because it could be considered plagiarism. If however, the photographs provide *only a perspective framework* for new and original design ideas, plagiarism is not an issue. Clearly, plagiarism is involved when a drawing done by another individual is traced without credit given or if a design is lifted in totality and traced. Many professional illustrators and renderers keep a huge file of photographs of human figures, furnishings, and other elements to be traced into drawings. A light table makes any job of tracing very easy.

COMPUTER-GENERATED IMAGERY

Computer imaging of photographic images is increasingly popular with interior designers. There are a number of computer software programs available that allow for photographic imaging and manipulation. Some popular programs, such as Adobe Photoshop™ and Adobe Illustrator™, allow for photographs to be scanned, manipulated, and compiled. Multiple images that previously existed independently can be brought together and edited to create single images of a proposed design (Figures 4-9 and 4-10 were created through scanning and manipulation). A blend of imaging and illustration software can be used, allowing for photomontage, drawing, any painting within a single image. Small, medium-size, and large design firms are currently using this technology.

Digital cameras are available that capture, edit, and store images without the use of photographic film and chemicals. With the use of photographic manipulation software, images from digital cameras can be manipulated within seconds of capture. Currently, these cameras are expensive and are rarely used in day-to-day interior design practice. Given the rapid progress of technology, digital cameras may be embraced by environmental designers as cameras become affordable. Specialized photo imaging and illustration software and digital cameras are technologies that allow for creation of web pages and other forms of electronic publication useful for design communication.

Increasingly, architectural and interior designers are using CADD (computer aided drafting and design) in the creation of paraline and perspective drawings. Some software allows CADD-generated orthographic projections to be fairly easily converted into three-dimensional views. In other cases the three-dimensional image must be built separately, and this can be time-consuming. Currently, many of the more sophisticated three-dimensional drawing programs are difficult to learn to use. Yet once the data is correctly entered, various three-dimensional views are easily generated and changes are made with great ease. The location and height of the viewer are easily changed, allowing a range of drawings to be created.

CADD-generated three-dimensional images are highly accurate and provide great flexibility because changes can be made quickly. Today's CADD software ranges a great deal in price and sophistication, but rapid advances in CADD technology promise lower costs and greater sophistication in the future. CADD is currently used by designers in all areas of practice, from library design to kitchen and bath renovation. With future advances and refinement CADD-generated

Figure 4-9
Computer-generated image using hand-drawn elements manipulated with Photoshop™. Drawing by Cory Sherman and the author.

Figure 4-10
This hand-drawn image (see Figure 4-1) was scanned and manipulated to include signage. This is a very simple method of image manipulation achieved by using QuarkXPress 3.1.™

Figure 4-11
A computer-generated perspective drawing of the project featured in the professional case study (see Figures C-49 to C-58). Design and Drawing by Meyer, Scherer & Rockcastle Ltd.

imagery will continue to revolutionize interior design practice. Figure 4-11 is a computer-generated perspective drawing.

Many CADD three-dimensional views are generated as wire frames. Wire frames look similar to hand-drawn perspective sketches with construction lines running in all directions. Some of these lines can be hidden to more clearly depict an environment. Even so, wire frames can look somewhat unnatural, because items often do not appear as true three-dimensional solids until they are rendered.

In CADD-generated three-dimensional views, rendering is often handled as a second step in the drawing process, much as it is in hand drawing. The most elegant rendering of surface materials, color, value, and shadow is done with sophisticated software. Much of this software requires that the CADD-generated three-dimensional view be imported into the secondary rendering application. CADD-generated three-dimensional views can also be animated and used in multimedia presentations.

In current practice the largest and most specialized firms are using the most sophisticated three-dimensional computer imaging. However, many small and medium-size firms currently employ some type of computer-generated three-dimensional imagery. More information on computer rendering can be found in Chapter 5.

REFERENCES

Ching, Frank. *A Visual Dictionary of Architecture*. New York: John Wiley & Sons, 1995.

Ching, Frank. *Architectural Graphics*. New York: John Wiley & Sons, 1996.

Drpic, Ivo. *Sketching and Rendering Interior Space*. New York: Whitney Library of Design, 1988.

Forseth, Kevin, and David Vaughn. *Graphics for Architecture*. New York: John Wiley & Sons, 1980.

Hanks, Kurt, and Larry Belliston. *Rapid Viz*. Los Altos, CA: William Kaufman, 1980.

McGarry, Richard, and Greg Madsen. *Marker Magic: The Rendering Problem Solver for Designers*. New York: John Wiley & Sons, 1993.

Pile, John. *Perspective for Interior Designers*. New York: Whitney Library of Design, 1985.

Porter, Tom. *Architectural Drawing*. New York: John Wiley & Sons, 1990.

Rendering

INTRODUCTION TO RENDERING

Rendering visually enhances drawings. Rendering line drawings makes them more easily understood and allows for greater visual communication in design presentations. Rendering is often done to convey depth and to allow a two-dimensional drawing surface to appear more three-dimensional, thus revealing the material qualities of forms.

Because it can help clients understand a project, rendering is useful as a means of communication. However, some project budgets and schedules do not allow time for highly detailed renderings, whereas other projects require extensive, detailed rendering. This means that projects have different presentation parameters, requiring a range of rendering skills—from quick and loose to accurate and refined.

The level of rendering is also influenced by the phase of the design process in which the presentation takes place. For example, during the preliminary stages of design it is wise to keep renderings loose and sketchy in order to avoid having the project pinned down prematurely. It is best to consider carefully the audience and purpose for a rendering before beginning the actual rendering.

Many students approach rendering with fear and lack of self-confidence. However, an understanding of basic rendering concepts and techniques can allow designers and students to enhance a visual presentation significantly. There are dozens of rendering techniques, materials, and tools available. Practice, study, and the use of reference material can help designers to develop a personal system of rendering.

This chapter covers some basic concepts, materials, and techniques and is meant as an overview of rendering. Orthographic drawings are rendered differently than perspective drawings and, for that reason, are covered separately in this chapter. Paraline drawings are rendered in a manner similar to perspective drawings and are are thus not discussed separately.

RENDERING AS ILLUMINATION

The most important thing to understand about rendering is that regardless of style, rendering introduces qualities of illumination to a drawing. This means that good rendering introduces light into a drawing, making it appear more natural and creating the illusion of three dimensions. Rendering requires consideration of the light source, or sources, found in the environment and the resulting value relationships. This is true for quick sketches and elaborate illustrations, for colored and noncolored renderings. I believe considering the illumination in a rendering is perhaps the single most important aspect of rendering.

Simply stated, light falls on an object and illuminates its surfaces to varying degrees. The type of lighting, the location of the light source(s), and the object's material qualities all affect

Figure 5-1

This cube is rendered to illustrate value. The top of the cube is light because it is receiving direct light from the light source. Shade (found on the sides of the cube) occurs in those areas not receiving light directly. Shadows are created on the surfaces blocked from receiving light. These varying degrees of light and shade are referred to as VALUE. All good rendering is based on value relationships. The front edge of the cube is called the LEADING EDGE and is drawn in white.

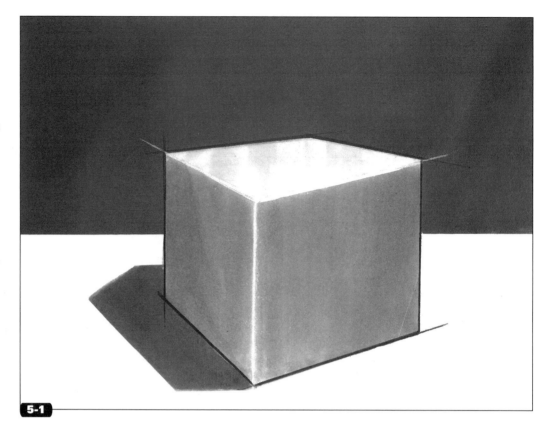

5-1

the manner in which the object is illuminated. Without consideration of the light source(s) and the related value relationships, renderings always look like something out of a child's coloring book

As a light source illuminates an object, it creates varying degrees of light on the object's surfaces. Those areas that receive direct light become the light areas of the object. Shade occurs in those areas not receiving light directly. Shadows are created on the surfaces blocked from receiving light. These varying degrees of light and shade are referred to as **VALUE**. All good rendering is based on value relationships. Figure 5-1 illustrates light, shade, and shadow.

MATERIALS, MEDIA, AND TOOLS

The list of materials and tools used in rendering is long and continues to grow. Professional illustrators and renderers employ many methods, use a range of supplies, and generally have distinct personal preferences. An understanding of materials and techniques allows a designer to make wise decisions and work quickly. This means that a basic understanding of materials and media is important. In rendering there are no hard and fast rules—anything goes. Great rendering requires exploration and curiosity about how materials will work in a given situation. Figure C-1 depicts a range of rendering media, materials, and tools; Figure C-2 gives examples of various rendering surfaces and media.

Because there are no absolute rules in rendering, it is wise to do a good deal of casual research. Looking at good rendering, fine art, and illustration is essential. To this end, books, periodicals, exhibitions, and visits to design firms are useful. Looking at what works in a successful painting or pastel drawing can teach a great deal about how to work with color markers. Discussions with art supply store personnel can be valuable in acquiring information about paper, drawing surfaces, and other supplies.

PAPER AND DRAWING SURFACES

The type of paper or rendering surface used has a significant influence on the quality of the final product. Many designers limit themselves to working on tracing paper or vellum because these papers are commonly used throughout the design process and are available in design offices.

Tracing paper and vellum have slick surfaces and are transparent, allowing them to be overlaid and easily traced. Graphite pencils, ink pens, and colored pencils and markers are often used with success on tracing paper and vellum. Markers are not absorbed into the surface of these papers, so the color stays rather weak and tends to pool. This creates softer color renderings that often have a watercolor effect, which can be attractive. Colored pencil can be layered on top of marker on these transparent papers to enrich the color and define edges. Using a combination of white, beige/cream, and darker pencils for highlights and refinement can work particularly well. On tracing paper and vellum white gouache works well for tiny areas of highlight.

MARKER, or VISUALIZING PAPER is commonly used in advertising and industrial design and is excellent for rich marker renderings. Marker paper is less transparent than tracing paper or vellum but absorbs markers very well (see Figures C-6 and C-7). Graphite, ink pens, colored pencils, and small amounts of paint (including gouache) can all work well on marker paper. Some heavier types of marker paper may be difficult to see through and require the use of a light table or taping onto a sunny window for tracing. Some types of marker paper can be photocopied and rendered. Pretesting of paper, photocopier toner, and marker compatibility is required. Figure 5-2 is a rendering on marker paper.

Plain BOND PAPER, used in standard office copying machines, is highly absorbent and can be used for rendering. Bond paper can be very messy because it soaks up marker dye, but when used with care it can create rich marker renderings. This paper also allows colored pencils to be layered over marker for clarity, crispness, and highlights. Rendering directly on bond photocopies is a fast, popular rendering technique that is becoming the standard in design offices. A word of caution: some marker base components can smear and dissolve copy toner, resulting in disaster.

Marker paper and bond paper allow for mistakes to be carefully cut out and reworked; problem areas can be replaced with new

WALL SCONCE   OVERHEAD DINING LIGHT   SIDE TABLE LAMP

5-2

Figure 5-2
A rendering created on marker
paper.
Drawing, rendering by Michael
Andreini.

portions. In addition, objects with ragged, poorly rendered edges can be cleanly cut and placed on a new sheet of paper. This technique works particularly well with photocopies and is used a great deal in product rendering.

There are many types of nontransparent paper that are used in rendering. These papers require some method of image transfer. TRANSFER PAPER, available from art supply stores, is placed between the original image and the rendering surface; the image is then redrawn and, thus, transferred. A cheap alternative method involves drawing on the back of the original with a soft pencil. The original is then placed face up on the rendering surface, and the image is redrawn, causing it to transfer. With some types of paper, commercial photocopying machines are also effective in reproducing images.

A variety of nontransparent colored papers can work well for stylized, minimally rendered presentations. Canson™ paper and other types of pastel paper accept graphite, ink, marker, colored pencil, pastel, and small amounts of gouache. This type of colored paper works best when the color selected is used in great amounts in the final rendering. For example, an interior with green slate used abundantly as a finish material can be very nicely rendered on similarly green-colored Canson paper. With the appropriate paper color selected, only the highlights, darkest values, and shadows are rendered in, leaving the paper color to serve as the middle value of the rendering (see Figures C-15 and C-16).

Many colored papers are highly textured on one side only. Colored pencils used on the highly textured side create a grainy look. Sometimes this is not desirable, so care must be taken in selecting the best side for rendering. Some types of colored papers can be photocopied, allowing for speed in the rendering process. However, tests should be run prior to rendering because copy toner does not adhere

Figure C-1

Rendering media, materials, and tools.

1. Spray fixative
2. Transfer paper
3. Glue stick
4. Gouache and brush
5. Removable tape
6. Rubber cement
7. Acrylic gesso
8. Rubber cement thinner
9. Cotton pad (for use with thinner and pastels)
10. Marker blender
11. Vellum
12. Marker paper
13. Illustration board
14. Black mounting board
15. Canson™ paper
16. Museum board
17. Handmade paper
18. Kraft paper
19. Watercolor paper (hot press)
20. Watercolor paper (cold press)
21. Ink pens
22. Snap-off cutter
23. Colored pencils (wax based)
24. Dry pastels
25. Pastels scraped into powder
26. Baby powder (for use with pastel powder)
27. Studio markers
28. Marker refill
29. Watercolor brushes
30. Watercolor paint

Figure C-2

Matrix showing examples of various rendering surfaces and media.

1. Graphite
2. Ink
3. Wax-based colored pencil (color)
4. Wax-based colored pencil (white)
5. Studio marker (colored)
6. Studio marker (gray)
7. Dry pastel (powder)
A. Vellum
B. Tracing paper
C. Drafting film
D. Marker paper
E. Bristol paper
F. Blueline diazo print paper
G. Canson paper (textured side)
H. Canson paper (smooth side)
I. Kraft paper
J. Bristol board
K. Museum board
L. Watercolor paper (cold press)
M. Illustration board (hot press)
N. Mat board
O. Black mounting board

Figures C-18a, C-18b
Student design development
presentation rendering on
bond paper with marker and
colored pencil.
Design and rendering by
Ardella Pieper.

Figure C-19
Rendering by a professional design illustrator for a preliminary design presentation. Marker, colored pencil, dry pastel, and white-out pen on marker paper.
Project: Casino.
Design: Smart Associates.
Illustration: Harris Birkeland.

C-19

Figure C-20
Rendering by a professional design illustrator for a design development presentation. Marker and colored pencil on bond paper. Notice the movement of color throughout the composition.
Project: Ward House at Winchester Gardens, Maplewood, New Jersey.
Design: Arthur Shuster Inc.
Illustration: Janet Lawson Architectural Illustration.

C-20

C-21a

Figure C-21a
A color and value study is a necessary step in successful rendering. Bond paper and marker.
Project: Period interior, the Royal Pavilion at Brighton, England.
By Leanne Larson.

Figure C-21b
Final rendering on bond paper with markers and colored pencil.
Project: Period interior, the Royal Pavilion at Brighton, England.
By Leanne Larson.

C-21b

Figure C-22a
Perspective rough-out using prepared grid. Notice that boxes are used as guides for drawing furnishings, fixtures, and architectural elements.
Project: University Church of Hope, Minneapolis, Minnesota.
Design: CNH Architects, Inc.
Drawing: Janet Lawson, Architectural Illustration.

C-22a

Figure C-22b
Final perspective rendering by a professional design illustrator. Marker on bond paper.
Project: University Church of Hope, Minneapolis, Minnesota.
Design: CNH Architects, Inc.
Illustration: Janet Lawson Architectural Illustration.

C-22b

Figure C-23a
Quick perspective study
created during schematic design.
Colored pencil on tracing paper.

Figure C-23b
Refined perspective rendering
created for a design development
presentation. Marker and black
ink on marker paper. Note that
glass is treated simply with
vertical strokes of light blue
marker.

C-24

Figure C-24
Rendered perspective included in student design development presentation. Marker and pencil on bond paper.
Design and rendering by Leanne Larson.

C-25

Figure C-25
Rendered perspective included in student design development presentation. Marker and pencil on bond paper. Notice the vertical application of marker and portions of paper left blank to serve as highlights.
Design and rendering by Susan Reische.

BACHELOR KITCHEN DESIGN

C-26

Figure C-26
Rendered perspective included in student schematic design presentation. Marker on bond paper. Note that a small icon of the floor plan is included to indicate direction of view. Design and rendering by Leanne Larson.

C-27

ROLLING PIN RACK DETAIL

C-28

Figure C-27
Rendered perspective included in student schematic design presentation. Marker, colored pencil, and ink on Canson paper, with bond paper insert. Note that a small icon of the floor plan is included to indicate direction of view.
Design and rendering by Ardella Pieper.

Figure C-28
Rendered perspective and design details included in a student design development presentation. Note that the floor plan is used as a project graphic in the title area. Marker, ink, and colored pencil on bond paper. Design and rendering by Kelly Urevig.

C-29

Figure C-29
Computer-generated image of a
bank lobby.
Software: ArchiCAD[a] 5,
Artlantis[a] 2.1, Canvas[a] 5.
Project: Citizens State Bank,
Cadott, Wisconsin.
By David Lien & David Peterson
Architects Inc.
Rendering by Aj Dumas.

Figure C-30
Computer-generated image of a
worship space.
Software: Architrion 5.8,
Artlantis 2.1, Canvas 5.
By David Lien & David Peterson
Architects Inc.
Rendering by Aj Dumas.

C-30

C-31

C-32

Figures C-31, C-32
Images taken from a professional multimedia design presentation. Project: New Headquarters Facility, Middle East. Software: AES™ (Architect/Engineer Software), 3-D Studio Max™R3, Photoshop™ 4.0, Autocad™ R 12. By Ellerbe Becket, Minneapolis. Project Team: Jerry Croxdale, Robert Herrick, Dave Koenen, Chris Mullen, Prasad Vaidya, and Jeffrey Walden.

Figure C-33
Professional computer-generated image.
Project: Wilsons the Leather Experts.
Software: FormZ™ (modeling), and Electric Image Animation System™ (rendering).
Designed, computer modeled, and rendered by Craig Beddow, Beddow Design • Digital Architecture. Courtesy of Wilson the Leather Experts.

Figure C-34
Professional computer-generated image.
Project: Wilsons the Leather Experts.
Software: FormZ (modeling), and Electric Image Animation System (rendering).
Designed, computer modeled, and rendered by Craig Beddow, Beddow Design • Digital Architecture. Courtesy of Wilson the Leather Experts.

Figure C-35
Professional computer-generated image (photo merge).
Project: Wilsons the Leather Experts.
Software: FormZ™ (modeling and rendering), Adobe Photoshop™ (compositing and image manipulation).
Designed, computer modeled, and rendered by Craig Beddow, Beddow Design • Digital Architecture. Courtesy of Wilson the Leather Experts.

Figure C-36
Study model for a corporate headquarters. Foam board, plastic, teak veneer, metal mesh, fabric.
Design and model by Meyer, Scherer & Rockcastle Ltd.

C-37

Figure C-37
Presentation model for a
corporate headquarters.
Basswood.
Design and model by Meyer,
Scherer & Rockcastle Ltd.

Figure C-38
Professional presentation
board. Mounted on foam board,
titles on plastic label tape,
hand-drawn ink borders.
Project: Laurel Gardens
of Avon, Avon, Connecticut.
By Arthur Shuster Inc.

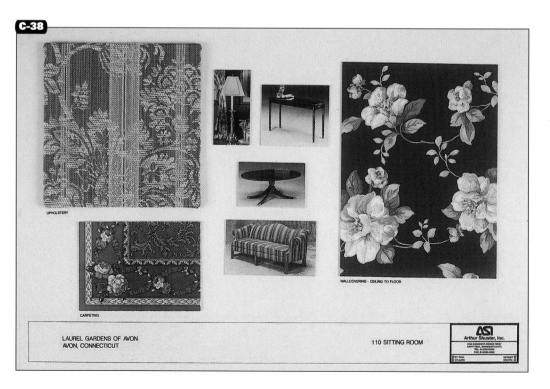

C-38

UPHOLSTERY

WALLCOVERING - CEILING TO FLOOR

CARPETING

LAUREL GARDENS OF AVON
AVON, CONNECTICUT

110 SITTING ROOM

Arthur Shuster, Inc.

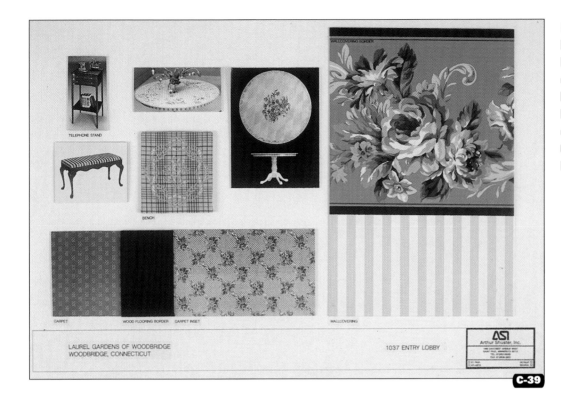

Figure C-39
Professional presentation board.
Mounted on foam board, titles
on plastic label tape,
hand-drawn ink borders.
Project: Laurel Gardens
of Woodbridge, Woodbridge,
Connecticut.
By Arthur Shuster Inc.

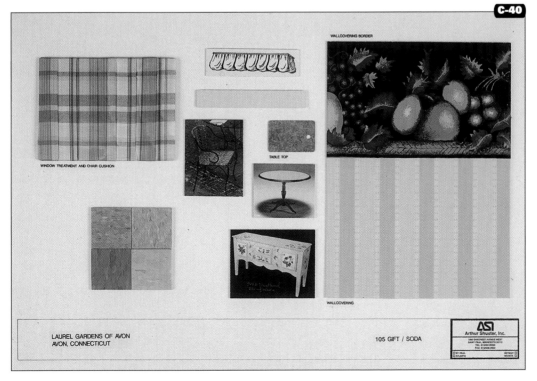

Figure C-40
Professional presentation
board. Mounted on foam board,
titles on plastic label tape,
hand-drawn ink borders.
Project: Laurel Gardens
of Avon, Avon, Connecticut.
By Arthur Shuster Inc.

Figure C-41

Professional presentation board. Mounted on foam board, titles on plastic label tape, hand-drawn ink borders. Project: Lourdes Nursing Home, Waterford, Michigan. By Arthur Shuster Inc.

Figure C-42

Professional presentation board. Mounted on foam board, titles on plastic label tape, hand-drawn ink borders. Project: Lourdes Nursing Home, Waterford, Michigan. By Arthur Shuster Inc.

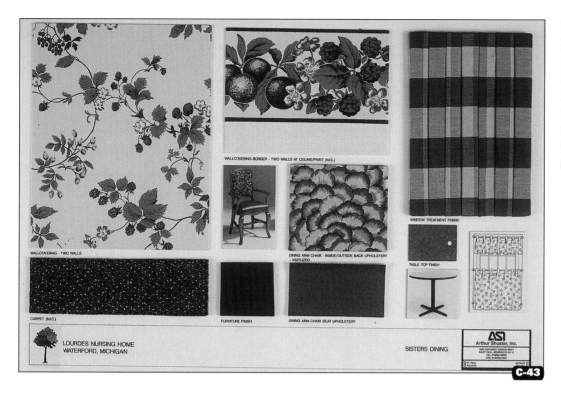

Figure C-43
Professional presentation board. Mounted on foam board, titles on plastic label tape, hand-drawn ink borders.
Project: Lourdes Nursing Home, Waterford, Michigan.
By Arthur Shuster Inc.

Figure C-44
Conceptual design presentation, exploring material culture. Constructed of found objects, paper, mounted on wood.

Figure C-45
Student design development presentation. Samples mounted on photocopied Canson paper, rendered in marker.
By Kelly Urevig.

Figure C-46
Student design development presentation. Samples mounted on handmade paper, plan and text photocopied on kraft paper. By Ardella Pieper.

Figure C-47
Two portfolio pages making use of a consistent grid format. By Kelly Urevig.

C-48a

C-48b

Figure C-48a, C-48b
Preliminary conceptual
sketches (droodles). Marker,
colored pencil, and ink on
watercolor paper.
Drawings by Thom Lasley
Courtesy of Thom Lasley

C-49

Case Study 1: Science Museum of Minnesota
Designer Thom Lasley began his work on this project, a large multilevel museum facility, by creating preliminary "droodles," or design doodles (Figures C-48a and C-48b). Lasley sought to create order within the huge volume of space and to create an "experience of exhibits." This was accomplished by employing the concept of a game board as a design metaphor and ordering spaces as they would be in a dynamic city.

Lasley then worked with Harris Birkeland, a professional design illustrator, to clarify and communicate the design with colored, conceptual, preliminary sketches. Birkeland's sketches were used as a means of communicating the spirit of the design to the client early in the design process (Figures C-49, C-50, C-51, C-52, C-53, and C-54).

Interior designer Jane Rademacher researched and selected a wide range of materials and finishes, which were presented on large, dynamic boards (Figures C-55, C-56, C-57, and C-58). The conceptual sketches, materials boards, and CADD-generated floor plans were presented together in preliminary conceptual design presentations. Preliminary CADD floor plans can be found in Appendix 3.

Figures C-49, C-50, C-51, C-52, C-53, C-54
Colored conceptual sketches, created in mixed media including marker paper, colored paper, markers, dry pastel, and white-out pen.
Sketches by Harris Birkeland.
Courtesy of Ellerbe Becket and the Science Museum of Minnesota.

C-50

C-51

C-52

C-53

C-54

Figure C-55, C-56, C-57, C-58 Presentation boards. On Gator Board. Boards prepared by Jane Rademacher, logos by the Ellerbe Becket graphic design staff. Photographs by Peter Lee. Courtesy of Ellerbe Becket and the Science Museum of Minnesota.

Figures C-59 to C-68
Architecture, interior design, models, renderings, drawings, and boards by Meyer Scherer & Rockcastle Ltd.

Case Study 2: Financial Corporation Headquarters

This project involved the design of a new corporate campus for 700 occupants. The client wanted a design that was revolutionary in terms of work process and flexibility, was technologically advanced, and made use of environmentally responsible materials.

The designers sought to create elements of visual consistency that could be shared by the various buildings, and at the same time create buildings with distinct identities. Project interior designer, Lynn Barnhouse, began the process with "inspiration boards" as a means of defining color identities for each building (Figures C-59 and C-60). Based on the inspiration boards and further study, preliminary materials boards were made and presented for each building (Figures C-61 and C-62), as were colored drawings (Figures C-63 and C-64). Later, finalized materials boards were presented (Figure C-65).

Scale models were used to study interior spatial relationships as well as specialized furnishings and equipment. (Figures C-66 and C-67), eventually full scale mock-ups were created to study interior details.

CADD generated perspective views were used to explore scale, sight lines (due to the chaotic nature of elements), floor pattern, building color, and spatial relationships (Figure C-68).

C-59

C-60

C-62

SPRING HALL

C-61

MEADOWLANDS HALL

MEADOWLAND HALL

C-63

SPRING HALL

C-64

MEADOWLANDS HALL

C-65

C-66

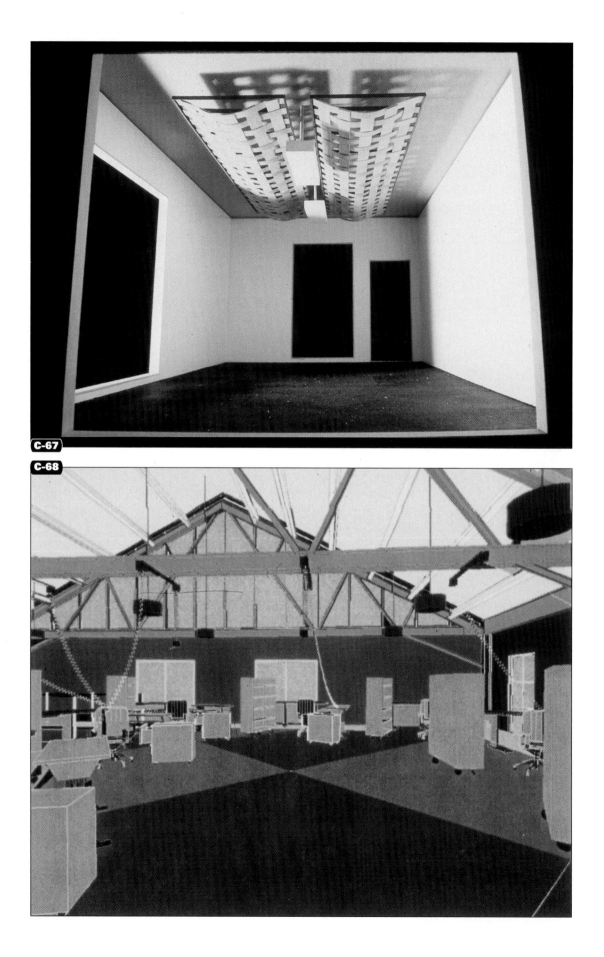

C-67

C-68

well to many types of colored paper.

Print paper used in diazo machines is also used for rendering. Because prints can be run quickly from an original, this method is highly efficient. Presentation BLUELINE, BLACKLINE, and sepia-toned prints are available at commercial blueprint shops and are easily rendered with marker and colored pencil. The choice of print paper is based on the colors used in the rendering. For example, a very warm rendering with a predominance of red, brown, or yellow is best rendered on brown- or black-toned print paper, but is difficult to render on blue-toned paper. Increasingly, large-format photocopying machines are replacing blueprint machines in popularity. Bond copies are highly absorbent, can offer rich renderings, and are commonly used in design offices for presentations.

Cheap brown KRAFT PAPER like the kind used for paper bags can also be used in rendering. Given the particular qualities of this paper, it should be used only in "earthy" or casual presentations. When used for the right project, this paper can work effectively. Kraft paper is highly absorbent and literally empties the dye out of a marker, which can be messy. Ink pen, colored pencil, and pastel work well on kraft paper to define edges and create highlights. Generally, this type of paper can be used in photocopying machines.

A variety of specialized art papers and hand-made papers can be used for rendering as well. These papers sometimes work in photocopying machines and are then rendered minimally for inclusion in a nontraditional presentation.

BRISTOL PAPER, BRISTOL BOARD, and ILLUSTRATION and MOUNTING BOARDS are, for the most part, highly absorbent and take markers very well. Many professional illustrators prefer illustration board for rendering. Bristol paper comes in a variety of weights, the thinnest of which work in photocopying machines. Illustration and some mounting boards are available in hot press (smoother, less tooth) and cold press (more textured, more tooth). Both hot and cold press boards absorb marker dye well. However, the texture of cold press products can create problems in detailed renderings. Colored pencils and ink pens can look unduly grainy on highly textured surfaces. Museum board is a beautiful, expensive, buttery soft board that comes in white, beige, gray, and black, is highly absorbent, and works well with colored pencil.

Drafting films are sometimes used in rendering. Generally, these films are nonabsorbent and tend to pool marker dye and ink. Graphite and colored pencils are sometimes used on drafting film. Paint works well on plastic film but requires hours of practice to master.

WATERCOLOR PAPER is used in working with wet media such as watercolor paint. Watercolor paper is available in hot or cold press, in finishes that range from smooth to very rough, and in various weights. Heavier weight paper is required in working without premounting the paper to a frame. Lighter weight paper should be presoaked with water, stretched, and taped or stapled to a sturdy frame. Watercolor paper absorbs marker dye readily and can be worked with graphite, ink, colored pencil, acrylic and gouache paint, and just about anything else commercially available for mark making. Heavily textured watercolor papers are very difficult to use for detailed design renderings.

RENDERING MEDIA

A trip to an art supply store makes evident the huge selection of rendering media, from colored pencils to markers and paint. The available rendering media range in price and have advantages and disadvantages. This means that no one item does everything well. For this reason most renderings require the use of more than one medium, and many renderings require a little bit of everything.

Graphite pencils, lead holders, and mechanical pencils can be used in noncolored renderings. As stated in Chapter 1, graphite pencils and leads are available in a range from soft to hard. This range allows great control over the quality of stroke laid down on the paper surface, resulting in variety, subtlety, and contrast. Pencils can be used for contour lines as well as texture, pattern, and material indication. Although pencil can be used to create subtle and beautiful original drawings and renderings, it does not reproduce as well as ink. This means that blueprints and photocopies of pencil renderings depicting variations of value and texture are often less clear than the original. Individual, deliberate pencil strokes reproduce far better than do those portions where the side of the pencil has been used to cover large areas. In cases where a rendering will be heavily reproduced, pencil may be a poor choice.

Ink used in refillable or disposable pens creates excellent line work that reproduces beautifully in both photocopying and diazo machines. Thus, ink can be used successfully to create line drawings for reproduction and overrendering with colored media.

Unfortunately, using ink can be messy and time-consuming. Before ink dries, it can smear and ruin an original. Therefore, it is wise to take care with ink drawings and use ink only as the final step in drawings that have been fully drawn with guidelines in graphite, nonphoto, or nonprint pencil. Inking triangles with raised edges are also helpful.

Refillable technical pens in varying widths are available, as are disposable ink pens. Refillable pens produce the finest quality of line, but they require cleaning and proper maintenance. Disposable ink pens are less consistent in terms of line quality, yet are preferred by some because they do not require cleaning or maintenance. Fine-point markers and various forms of felt-tip pens can be used to create excellent ink renderings. Disposable technical pens are useful in creating line drawings, whereas felt-tip ink markers work well on colored renderings to define edges.

There are three types of COLORED PENCILS: wax based, oil based, and water soluble. I find the wax-based the most useful in rendering. In my experience, Berol Prismacolor™ wax-based pencils are the easiest to render with. Colored pencils can work well alone, although for rich color buildup they must be layered or manipulated. See Figure C-3 for examples of colored pencil color manipulation. Without layering, colored pencils can look grainy because the pencil often works only on the top surface of the paper, allowing little valleys to stay uncolored. Underlayering warm colors with deep red pencil and cool colors with indigo blue pencil can diminish the grainy look.

A variety of solvents can be used to decrease the grainy quality of pencil renderings. One of the best is rubber cement thinner, which is toxic and emits vapors that can cause serious health problems. Use rubber cement thinner in an appropriate manner, and follow the warning instructions carefully. In using this solvent, a small amount is placed on a cotton swab and applied on top of colored pencil—in a well-ventilated space.

An alcohol-based colorless blender marker is an alternative pencil solvent that poses fewer health hazards. The colorless blender can be applied over the surface of the colored pencil area and worked back and forth, loosening up the pencil.

Often when used alone and overworked, wax-based pencils can produce a buildup of wax. This makes the area look very shiny, overdone, and amateurish. The solution to this shiny buildup is to apply a layer of color or gray marker before any pencil touches the paper. The marker works like a paint primer and allows the surface to accept pencil better. This works well when done with subtle shades of the object color or light values of gray. Coating paper with acrylic gesso also adds a primer coat for pencil renderings.

The appearance of colored pencil rendering varies greatly according to the type and texture of paper used, thus creating a need for experimentation. In addition, the way the pencil is held and the stroke used produces different effects. When used to cover large areas, colored pencils are best applied with angled strokes. Using strokes of roughly 45 degrees is less tiring and produces an attractive rendering. Pencils must be kept very, very sharp when used to define edges and outline objects. In creating outlines or definition, the use of a metal or plastic straightedge is required. Sharp pencils have a greater surface area and cover large areas rapidly.

Pencils can be used over marker renderings to enhance color and define shape and value. A sharp white or light-colored pencil works well to clean up messy edges of marker rendering. To create very subtle color variations, colored pencil pigment can be chipped away from the pencil, using a blade, and applied by rubbing onto the drawing surface with a tissue.

ART MARKERS, also called STUDIO MARKERS, are filled with transparent dye in an alcohol or xylene base solution. Xylene-based markers last longer and are considered by some to have better color rendition. Unfortunately, xylene-based markers produce fumes and can cause health problems. For this reason, some schools, institutions, and design firms have policies prohibiting the use of xylene-based art supplies.

Alcohol-based markers have recently improved greatly and are now widely used. Unfortunately, alcohol-based markers tend to dry up quickly and do not last long. Denatured alcohol or 91 percent alcohol solution can be used to revive markers. Marker tips can be removed and an alcohol solution placed in the marker body, or the marker can be placed (open) with the tip in an alcohol solution. Because they dry up quickly, alcohol-based markers should be tested prior to application on a final rendering; this prevents unwanted streaks and poor color matches.

There are numerous brands of high-quality art markers currently available. Many designers and illustrators have distinct personal favorites. Others tend to mix and match brands, based on availability, price, and color selection. Many of my students currently prefer Pantone Tria™ markers by Letraset™ because they have three tip sizes, produce good color rendition, and are refillable.

Markers are a popular rendering medium because they are quick to use, do not require extensive setup or cleaning time, and come in an enormous range of colors. However, markers can be difficult to master because they are difficult for beginners to control. Moreover, marker color must be manipulated to portray value, texture, and material qualities successfully.

When possible, marker strokes should be applied against a straightedge. Do not use metal or plastic edges for applying marker color, as it smears and causes problems. The best straightedge for marker application is a strip of mat or illustration board.

Marker color is usually layered or touched up with additional media in order to properly render value and color. A single marker color can be applied in layers to create value contrast. Gray marker as well can be layered under the appropriate color to create value or enrich color. Colored pencil, pastel, and small quantities of paint can be layered over marker color to create value contrast or tune up color. See Figure C-4 for examples of marker color manipulation.

Regardless of the method used, marker color must be manipulated to reveal form. The most common mistake in marker rendering is neglecting to manipulate marker color and, in so doing, creating "coloring book" images that appear amateurish. Often marker color is too intense for use in interior perspectives. One method for softening marker intensity is to use colorless blender to pick up the marker dye and then apply it to the drawing surface. To do this, apply the marker to slick paper, "pick it up" with the colorless blender, and apply it to the rendering surface (Figure C-5).

DRY PASTELS (sometimes called chalk) work well as a complement to marker and colored pencil renderings. These pastels are dry and chalky in contrast to oil pastels. Dry pastels can be used to color an area quickly and can create very light washes for highlights. One useful dry pastel technique involves using the edge of a blade to shave off portions of pastel, creating a pastel pigment dust. The pastel dust can be mixed with baby powder, making it easy to work. The dry pastel and baby powder mixture is then smoothed onto the rendering surface with tissue or cotton, over marker or alone, and used to create washes of color. Pastels are also blended into a drawing with a finger this works far better than simply drawing with a pastel stick.

Dry pastels work well on colored paper as a primary rendering medium, but are best used in less detailed renderings. Large areas of pastel can be applied neatly when worked against removable tape or sticky back as a masking agent. It is very easy to erase or brush pastels from a drawing surface. Finished pastel drawings require the application of fixative spray to keep them in place. This can cause problems in renderings done with markers in that fixative can remove marker dye. Special marker fixative is available if required.

WATERCOLORS, transparent water-based paints used by many professional illustrators and artists, can be used to create beautiful renderings. However, they are very difficult to use and are extremely time-consuming. A good deal of practice and experimentation is required in developing watercolor painting skills. Students interested in watercolor rendering are well advised to enroll in a watercolor painting course and use the information gained for future rendering.

Watercolor rendering requires special tools such as brushes, high-quality paper, and mounting board. Because it is time-consuming, watercolor rendering is not often used for preliminary or schematic presentations but is instead used in final design presentations.

GOUACHE is an opaque water-based paint. When used straight from the tube, gouache appears opaque. When mixed with water, gouache can become somewhat transparent. Professional illustrators and renderers use gouache to create rich, realistic renderings. However, like water-colors, gouache painting is time-consuming and requires special skills and equipment. Because it is water-based and is often mixed with water, gouache should be applied only to heavier papers.

White or light-colored gouache can be used to create highlights and glints on marker, ink, and pencil renderings. This is best done by mixing white gouache with a small amount of water and applying it to the drawing surface with a very fine paintbrush. The gouache should be applied with great care, in extremely small quantities only. When applied improperly, white gouache can appear unnatural and seriously distract from a rendering. It is advisable for students to keep a small tube of white gouache, as well as a very fine paintbrush, on hand for painting tiny highlights into some renderings.

An **AIRBRUSH** is actually a system that propels paint or dye onto a drawing surface. In standard airbrush systems a compressor, hose, and spray gun combine to propel the pigment. Airbrushes produce dazzling, sophisticated images with an amazing range of hue and value. Standard airbrush systems are expensive and require lots of practice. A great deal of setup and cleanup time is required for airbrush use.

There are airbrush attachments that can be purchased for use with markers. These are less costly and require less preparation time than traditional airbrushes. Marker airbrush attachments require plenty of practice and generally involve masking off large areas of a drawing. I have found them to produce inconsistent results.

Many renderings combine various forms of media. It is common to see renderings created with marker, colored pencil, a bit of pastel, ink, and tiny areas of paint. The combining of media limits weaknesses and takes advantage of strengths. Some designers are cre-

Figure 5-3
A floor plan with simplified shadows, all cast at a consistent 45 degrees.

ating renderings that are collages of a variety of materials and media and come from a range of sources (see Figure C-8). Some collages make use of computer-generated images combined with hand-drawn images (see Figure 4-9).

Other successful collages are hand rendered, with the exception of photographs of human figures and entourage elements. For the most part these collages create nontraditional renderings that may not be appropriate for all projects. With the audience and project carefully considered, nontraditional collage-type renderings can successfully communicate conceptual as well as spatial issues.

RENDERING ORTHOGRAPHIC PROJECTION DRAWINGS

Rendering orthographic projections helps to reveal the material qualities of the design and indicate relative depth. Because orthographic views are by nature flattened views, they often require rendering as a means of graphic enhancement. With the appropriate enhancement, orthographic views can be used successfully in design presentations. This is fortunate, because orthographic views are created on most projects and are therefore readily available for use in design presentations. For this reason, rendered orthographic views are commonly used for presentations made throughout the design process. Orthographic projections are faster and easier to render than perspective drawings.

The best way to begin a rendered plan, section, or elevation is to create a clean original drawing. In order for the final rendering to have clarity, complex dimensions and confusing notes should be omitted. Items such as ceramic tile and certain simple textures may exist on the original drawing or can be drawn in as part of the rendering process.

The key to rendering is to consider light, and this is most easily accomplished in orthographic projections by adding shadows. If time allows, additional value contrast, material, and color rendition can be included in the rendering. Including shadows helps to reveal height and can provide the contrast necessary to enhance the drawing. There are a number of methods for determining shadow location and length; most of these are overcomplicated. Quite often, shadows can be simplified and estimated with few ill effects.

SIMPLIFIED SHADOWS IN PLAN DRAWINGS

There are two simple systems for estimating shadows in plan drawings. One system employs a consistent shadow orientation for the entire plan. Typically, this simplified system employs a 45-degree diagonal direction for the light source. Each element and object in the entire plan receives a shadow cast by the same 45-degree light source. Shadows are drawn adjacent to each form in plan at a 45-degree angle, using a standard 45-degree triangle. The length of each shadow is estimated based on the relative height of each form. This method is simple and creates an easy-to-read plan (Figure 5-3).

Another shadow estimation system involves creating shadows that are cast by the variety of light sources found in the environment. The locations of windows, skylights, and electric light sources are used to cast 45-degree shadows. This system creates shadows that vary from room to room, relative to the natural and electric light sources. Shadows are cast at 45-degree angles (using a 45-degree triangle), based on the location of the light source. Shadow length is estimated relative to height. This variable shadow system creates dramatic effects that help to indicate window locations (Figure 5-4). However, plans employing this system require more time, and complex plans can be visually confusing.

SIMPLIFIED SHADOWS IN ELEVATION AND SECTION DRAWINGS

Shadows enhance elevations and sections. In these drawings they can be used to indicate the relative depths and the forms of design elements. A simple technique is for shadows to be drawn in section and elevation as cast from top right to bottom left, following a 45-degree diagonal, thus allowing for the use of a standard 45-degree triangle.

In elevation, shadows are cast at 45 degrees with lengths determined by the relative depth of the object casting the shadow (Figure 5-5). Shadows drawn in elevation enhance a drawing but should generally be kept minimal in terms of length for purposes of graphic clarity. Where a dramatic rendering is required, shadows can be drawn with great lengths to create interest. It is important to note that exterior elevations, unlike interiors, are often drawn with dramatic shadows this is because they are outdoors, receiving large quantities of natural light.

Figure 5-4
A floor plan with simplified
shadows, cast at 45 degrees,
based on natural light direction.

Figure 5-5
An interior elevation with
simplified shadows, cast at
45-degree angles.

Section drawings have shadows cast by cut elements such as the roof, floors, and walls. Generally, the length of these shadows is varied, based on the distance from the cutline to the plane receiving the shadow.

TEXTURE, PATTERN, AND MATERIAL QUALITIES

It is often useful to render the material properties of design elements in orthographic projection drawings. This is done by delineating the size and location, texture and finish of both building elements and furnishings. Rendering these elements in plan and elevation drawings is easier and less time consuming than rendering in perspectives and paraline drawings. For this reason, it is not unusual to see professional design presentations that consist of rendered plans and elevations and nonrendered perspective drawings. When such elements are drawn

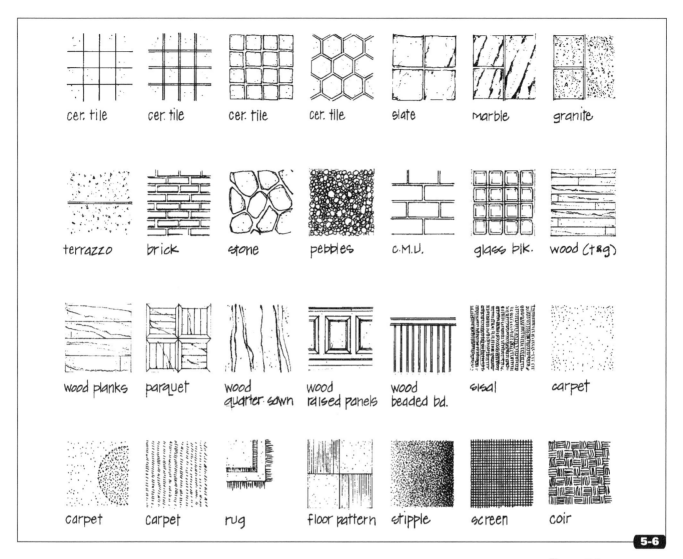

Labels within the figure:

cer. tile   cer. tile   cer. tile   cer. tile   slate   marble   granite

terrazzo   brick   stone   pebbles   c.m.u.   glass blk.   wood (t&g)

wood planks   parquet   wood quarter sawn   wood raised panels   wood beaded bd.   sisal   carpet

carpet   carpet   rug   floor pattern   stipple   screen   coir

5-6

Figure 5-6
Examples of rendered finish materials for use in orthographic projections. NOTE: These are not the standard symbols for use in construction documents.

successfully, many clients can distinguish material qualities quite well in rendered orthographic projections.

Rendering materials and finishes can be done quite simply for example, with minimal line work and stippling used to indicate wood and ceramic tile. When necessary, great detail can be added to plans and elevations. There are some fairly standard conventions for rendering common finish materials in orthographic projection. See Figure 5-6 for examples of orthographic finish materials.

Regardless of the level of detail required for a given project, materials must be rendered in scale and with some indication of texture or surface finish. For example, the most minimally rendered plan should show properly scaled tile locations, wood floors in scale with a slight graining pattern, and minimal stippling for carpet locations. The indication of surface finishes in proper scale allows the plan to indicate accurately the finish material sizes and locations.

When in doubt about the rendering of a particular material, it is best to carefully examine the actual material and render an abstraction of what is visible. For example, no convention exists for rendering a speckled rubber floor tile. This particular tile can be rendered

Figure 5-7
Floor plan rendered with
disposable ink pens.

only through examination of its visual qualities. Are the speckles large or small? Are the speckles in a contrasting color? Are they random or in a particular pattern?

Some designers prefer spare, minimally rendered orthographic projections, whereas others prefer a detailed, rather busy style of rendering. This is certainly a matter of taste or personal style. Regardless of personal style, however, renderings of orthographic projections must be drawn in scale and should accurately reflect proportion and true material qualities. Figures 5-7, 5-8, and 5-9 are orthographic projections rendered with disposable ink pens.

Generally, accurate visual assessment of materials is a key to successful rendering. In some cases, certain materials simply cannot be rendered in the time allowed, and in those cases a legend system can be used to delineate material locations.

COLOR RENDERING PLANS, SECTIONS, AND ELEVATIONS

Prior to beginning any color rendering, a designer should consider the amount of time available and the nature of the project. Project phase, type of project, and the presentation audience are important factors in the selection of a color rendering style. All factors must be considered, and the most appropriate media chosen. Color rendering requires a working knowledge of color theory; some

Figure 5-8
Floor plan rendered with disposable ink pens.

Figure 5-9
Interior elevation rendered with disposable ink pens and marker.

basic color information can be found in Appendix 1.

Color rendering can greatly enhance plan, elevation, and section drawings. The quickest method calls for creating a photocopy or print of an original line drawing and rendering on the copy with pencil, marker, pastel, or a combination of these media (see Figures C-9, C-10a, C-10b, and C-11). Another quick method involves the use of white or colored tracing paper, laid over drawings and washed with colored pencil, ink, or washes of marker.

In working on bond copies and print paper, shadows can be rendered into the print with gray markers before the application of any colored marker or pencils. Areas that are to appear much darker in value should also be laid in gray marker prior to the application of color media. With shadows and darker values applied, marker color, pencil color, or pastels may then be used to create the desired hue. Because rendering on bond and print papers is quick and relatively easy, they are often used for design presentations, such as those made in the schematic design phase of a project. Figures C-12a, C-12b, C-2c, C-13a, C-13b, C-13c, C-14a, C-14b, and C-14c show the steps in rendering bond paper copies of plans and elevations.

Some varieties of colored paper can be photocopied and rendered. The color of paper selected will be predominant in the final rendering, and this should be considered. For example, selecting a paper color that is the middle value of a predominant color in

KITCHEN ELEVATION - EAST WALL

the design allows one to render only shadows, dark values, and highlights into those areas (see Figures C-15 and C-16).

In some cases, when little time is available, orthographic drawings can be spot rendered; this means that only a small portion (usually circular) of the drawing need be accurately rendered to indicate the materials used throughout the project (Figure C-17a). This technique is effective when the spot that is rendered clearly depicts the range of materials used in the project.

Another time-saving method involves using the correct color in a particular area and defining elements accurately in part of that area. For example, a large tile area can be indicated by applying the correct marker to the entire tiled portion, with only a limited number of tiles outlined in pencil, ink, or marker to show the tile size and shape (Figure C-17b). This allows the rendering to communicate material locations with a limited amount of detail work. This method must be accompanied by very clear verbal communication to allow clients to understand material locations.

TECHNIQUES AND TIPS

All rendered orthographic projections require shadows. Shadows should be considered prior to rendering, and a shadow plan should be created with each shadow located. Shadows can then be rendered in colored pencil, ink, or marker.

Because they can remove ink and colored pencil, markers should generally be used for a base coat. This means they should be applied before the use of ink or colored pencil. However, when necessary, light markers and colorless blenders can be used to remove areas of pencil that have become too waxy.

Plans, elevations, and sections require that large areas of marker be applied in deliberate strokes with a straightedge. Large areas of carpet or wood flooring should be applied with the lightest marker color possible, applied with a straightedge.

Additional layers of marker can be applied to tune up marker color and to add nuances where required. In rendering natural materials such as wood and stone, marker color should vary slightly; this requires going over particular areas with a second application of marker (Figures C-18a and C-18b).

Unsuccessful marker renderings of orthographic projections generally suffer from one or more of the following: strokes not created with a straightedge, marker color that is too intense, lack of value contrast (no highlights or dark values), or a combination of these flaws.

Colored pencil is often applied over gray or colored markers to add highlights, intensify dark areas, and to enrich color. Marker color alone is often too intense for use in interior renderings and requires the addition of colored pencil to soften and subdue the color.

Unsuccessful colored pencil renderings often suffer from heavy-handed use of a single color, pencil strokes that are all over the place, unsharpened pencil points, or a combination of all three.

RENDERING PERSPECTIVE DRAWINGS

Rendering perspective and paraline drawings is far more difficult and time-consuming than rendering orthographic projections. This is due to the complex nature of perspective drawing. Light, shade, and shadow must be rendered in perspective drawings. Moreover, the surfaces of objects recede toward vanishing points, creating complexity in rendering colors and materials. However, rendering adds richness, interest, and reality to perspective drawings, allowing for successful visual communication.

Rendered perspectives can help the proposed design to become real to a client and are thus excellent sales and communications tools. For this reason rendered perspectives are often used in formal final design presentations. There are many perspective rendering techniques, varying from those that can be accomplished quickly to those that require days for completion.

The time and budget constraints of a project influence the rendering method selected. When scheduling and budgets allow, professional illustrators may be hired to create highly detailed or dramatic renderings. Quickly drawn perspectives rendered with value and almost no color may be used on some projects. Sometimes minimally rendered black-and-white perspective drawings are used in tandem with rendered floor plans as these can be produced quickly. Because projects vary in terms of design fees and schedules, it is useful to be aware of a range of rendering techniques and basic perspective rendering concepts.

All rendering requires that the source of light and its influence on the environment be considered. In perspective rendering, however, light and its relationship to the object(s) rendered must be considered above all else. What is the light source or sources? How do the materials rendered react in relationship to the light source? Every stroke of the marker or pencil is actually determined by the relationship of light to the object.

Understanding the relationship of light, value, and shadow on basic forms in perspective is required for successful perspective rendering. The cube, cylinder, sphere, and cone are basic shapes that are found in combination in more complex objects. Learning to render these basic shapes in a variety of noncolor media is a useful preparation for the eventual rendering of color and materials. The basic shapes are most easily rendered with a light source above and slightly to the right or left. The light source in this position creates three distinct values (1) light value, (2) medium value, (3) dark value and (4) a cast shadow. Figure 5-10 illustrates this light source set up in relation to a variety of simple forms.

In this light source setup, the top surface of a cube receives the most light (value 1), followed by the side closest to the light source (value 2). The side farthest from the light source receives the least light and is darkest (value 3), and, typically, the cast shadow (4) is adjacent to the darkest side (see Figure 5-10).

A cylinder with this lighting setup has its top surface rendered as the lightest (value 1). Light curves around a curving surface, creating value contrasts that also curve around the cylinder. On a simplified, nonreflective cylinder, the portion of the cylinder closest to the light is rendered with the medium value (value 2) and the portion farthest from the light source is rendered the darkest value (value 3). The shadow (4) is generally located on the surface next to the darkest portion of the cylinder (see Figure 5-10).

Cylinders are frequently drawn in a more complex manner because they often pick up reflective light, causing a dark reflection next to the medium value of the cylinder, as well as a light reflection on the dark value. The portions of the cylinder farthest from the light source, which recede from the viewer, also receive medium to dark values. The location of the darkest value on a cylinder, cone, or sphere is called a CORE. Cores often have a thin reflected highlight immediately next to them.

A sphere with the described lighting setup has its top portion rendered as lightest (value 1), and as the surface curves away from the light source, values are blended in a range from medium (value 2) to dark (value 3). The shadow (4) is generally found on the surface next to the darkest portion of the sphere. Generally, values are rendered into a sphere with curved strokes that follow the form of the sphere. Often a bright highlight can be found toward the top portion of the sphere in the location of the lightest value. The darkest portion, or core, of a sphere is sometimes rendered with a narrow, adjacent highlight on reflective surfaces (see Figure 5-10).

A cone is rendered with the portion closest to the light source lightest (value 1), the center section of the cone rendered in middle value (value 2), and the portion of the cone farthest from the light receives the least light and is darkest (value 3). A shadow is most often found on the surface next to the darkest value of the cone. A cone with a reflective surface is rendered with the core, or darkest portion, adjacent to a highlight indicating surface reflection (see Figure 5-10).

It is essential to be able to render these basic forms with a minimum of three values. Complex, detailed rendering requires more value contrast to illustrate more complex lighting situations. However, a minimum of three values, plus a shadow, often allows a rendering to be visually successful.

RENDERING SHADOWS IN PERSPECTIVE DRAWINGS

In quick sketch renderings fewer values than the three discussed can be used in combination with rendered shadows. When time is scarce, a drawing can be slightly rendered by the inclusion of shadows only. There are a variety of methods of shadow construction, most of which are rather confusing and overtechnical. The important things to remember about shadows in perspective renderings are that shadows are absolutely necessary, especially on floor surfaces; shadows should be handled in a consistent fashion throughout the rendering; and shadows need not be

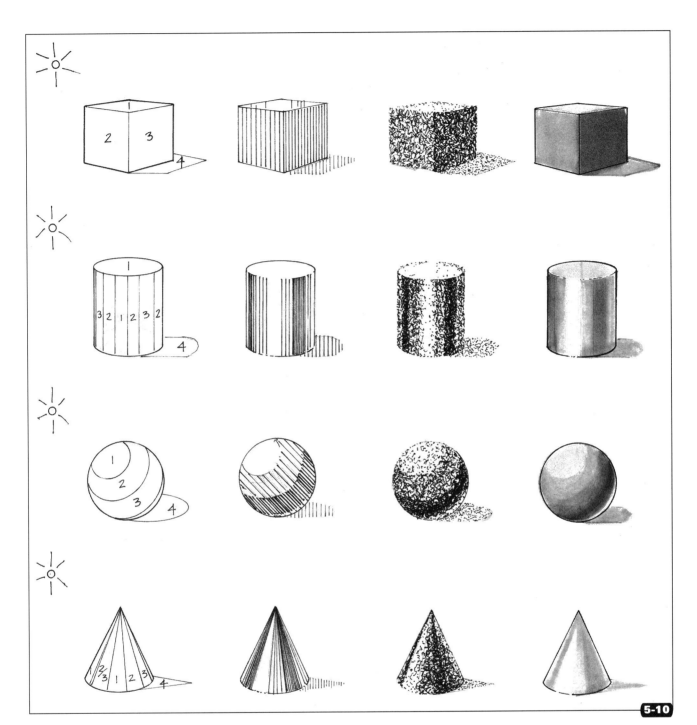

5-10

absolutely technically accurate to work well. Although shadows are necessary, they can be simplified and minimized for ease of rendering.

The easiest method of shadow construction employs sets of parallel lines that are cast as the bases of triangles. Shadows are constructed by selecting an angle formed by the light source and using this angle consistently to create a triangle from each corner of the object. The bases of the triangles are then connected to each other to form the shadow (Figure 5-11).

More dramatic shadows can be created by the use of a shadow vanishing point. This method requires that the light source be located

Figure 5-10
The basic shapes are most easily rendered with a light source above and slightly to the right or left. The light source in this position creates three distinct values—1, light value; 2, medium value; 3, dark value; and 4, cast shadow.

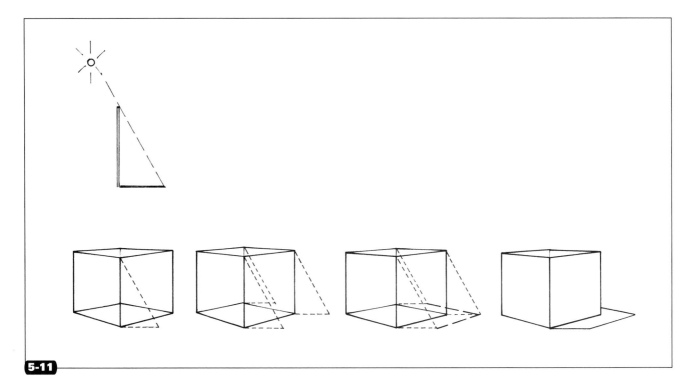

Figure 5-11
Quick reference: simple parallel
shadow construction.

Construct shadows by selecting
an angle formed by the light
source and using this angle
consistently to create triangles at
appropriate corners of the object.
The bases of the triangles are
then connected to one another to
form the shadow.

somewhere above the horizon line. A shadow vanishing point is then
plotted directly below the light source, on the horizon line. Lines are
drawn from the light source through the top corners of the object.
Lines are then drawn from the shadow vanishing point through the
bottom corners of the object. These two sets of lines form the shadow
location. The lines determining the length of the shadow are drawn
from the object's vanishing points through the shadow location,
depending on the overall length of shadow desired (Figure 5-12).

RENDERING PERSPECTIVE DRAWINGS WITHOUT COLOR

Most current reference books on rendering focus a great deal on
colored perspective drawings. It is useful, however, to learn to render
without color, because such renderings are quick and help one to
develop an understanding of value.

In noncolored renderings the type of marks made must be
appropriate to the surfaces being rendered and the rendering style.
For example, carpet is best rendered with stipples or tiny irregular
strokes, whereas polished metal is best rendered with gray markers or
ink washes. Messy scribbles and hatch marks look best on quick, freehand renderings. Detailed, refined renderings require lines drawn
with tools. The use of varying line weights can quickly define and
enhance a drawing. This is particularly true in outlining and defining
the overall form of an object.

The way the edges of an object are outlined can greatly enhance
the graphic quality of a quick rendering. The edges of an object that
lead toward the viewer are called leading edges. Leading edges are generally kept very light in line weight and are sometimes drawn in white
pencil or gouache. The edges of an object that recede away from the

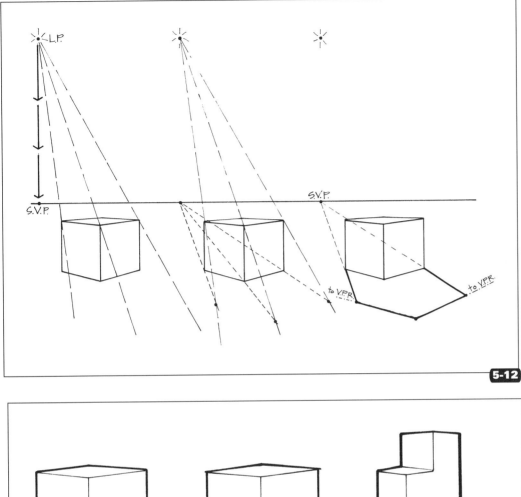

Figure 5-12
Quick reference: shadow construction with a shadow vanishing point (S.V.P.).

Decide on the location of the light source (L.P.). Plot a shadow vanishing point (S.V.P.) directly below the L.P. on the horizon line. Draw lines from the L.P. through the tops of the appropriate corners. Draw lines from the S.V. P. through the bottoms of the appropriate corners of the object. The lines determining the length of the shadows are drawn from the object vanishing points through the shadow locations, depending on the overall length of shadow desired.

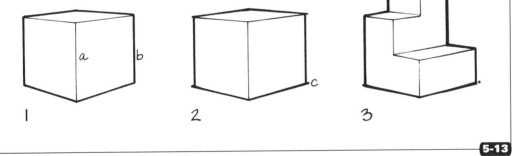

Figure 5-13
Leading and receding edges.
1. The edges of an object that lead toward the viewer are called leading edges; these edges are generally kept very light in line weight (a). The edges of an object that recede away from the viewer are called receding edges (b); these can be drawn in a very bold line to define the form of the object.
2. As lines recede, they can become bolder (c).
3. The use of leading and receding edges can quickly enhance a drawing.

viewer are sometimes called receding edges. Receding edges can be drawn in a very bold line weight to readily define the form of an object. The use of varying line weights to delineate leading and receding edges can greatly enhance a rendering. Figure 5-13 illustrates leading edges drawn with lines (see also Figure 5-1).

The best way to ensure that value and shadow relationships are included in every rendering is to create a value study prior to beginning the actual rendering. To create a value study, take a copy of the perspective line drawing and mark the values that will be rendered in each area. Shadows and highlights should be included (Figure 5-14a).

The three values and the shadow can be created without the introduction of color by using graphite pencils, ink pens or washes, markers, pastels, gray markers, or gray or white pencils. The values can be created using lines, scribble marks, hatching and cross-hatching,

Figure 5-14a
A value study is an important
first step in rendering a
perspective drawing.

5-14a

stippling, and shading by using the side of a pencil on edge. Marks made in ink will allow the best reproduction (Figures 5-14b and 5-14c).

Perspective drawings rendered with gray markers can work well in design presentations when combined with material sample boards or colored orthographic renderings. In addition, creating gray marker renderings can teach design students a great deal about value and marker application. For this reason, students should practice rendering with gray markers.

Gray marker renderings require that markers be applied with accurate and deliberate strokes. In most renderings the tops of horizontal surfaces are rendered in the lightest value, using very small amounts of marker. These lightest areas can have marker applied in circular strokes that are nondirectional. Also on these lightest surfaces, very light gray marker (10 to 20 percent gray) can be applied vertically or at an angle representing light reflection. For very light surfaces a dusting of gray pastel mixed with powder can be applied.

5-14b

Floors and walls of interior perspectives require special consideration concerning marker application. It is easiest to render walls by applying marker strokes vertically with a straight-edge (see Figure 5-15a). It is difficult to apply marker strokes horizontally or aiming toward a vanishing point, because the lines will overlap and distort the perspective.

A quick look at any floor surface will reveal many shadows, values, and highlights. No floor surface can be rendered by the application of a single marker layer applied consistently—this will look amateurish. Reflective and polished floors must be rendered with a range of lights, darks, and highlights (Figure 5-15b). Carpet must be rendered with a range of values, or it will appear flat and artificial.

Figure 5-14c
Value relationships can be
rendered using scribbles.

5-14c

Walls in most environments receive varying amounts of light,
this means that to work well in a rendering, walls must vary in value.
Typically, in one-point perspective the rear wall can be rendered in a
medium value with the two adjacent side walls rendered very light—or
not rendered at all (Figure 5-15b). In two-point perspective, one wall
can be slightly darker in value than the other to indicate a single light
source. Depending on the location of the light source(s), a single
wall plane may have variations in value. For example, those walls with
accent lights or sconces may be very light at the sources of light and
become darker as they recede from the light sources. See Figures C-
23a and C-23b for colored versions of Figure 5-15b.

Figures 5-15a, 5-15b
It is useful to apply marker with a straightedge. Markers used on wall and floor surfaces are often applied with a vertical stroke for the first layer; secondary layers can be applied free-hand.

Gray marker renderings are useful study tools and can be used in design presentations. Special care must be taken in these renderings to create value contrast, to include shadows, and to use a range of values on floor and wall surfaces. Markers should be carefully applied, and strokes should relate to the structure, form, or direction of an object. With these aspects considered, gray marker renderings can serve a valuable purpose.

Most noncolored renderings are created using combinations of the media mentioned here. Ink line work can be used to create value and indicate receding and leading edges, as can stipples. Gray markers used with black ink and gray and white colored pencils can clearly reveal the material qualities of form. With the introduction of minimal amounts of color, these drawings can be greatly enhanced.

COLOR RENDERING INTERIOR PERSPECTIVES

Adding color to renderings enhances design communication. It is best to think of color rendering as existing on a continuum, progressing from lightly rendered to fully rendered. Project constraints and the materials used often dictate the level of finish a color rendering will have. As with all aspects of design presentation, the designer must consider the audience, the conceptual issues, the phase of the design process, and the amount of time available. Color rendering requires a working knowledge of color theory; basic color information can be found in Appendix 1.

Colored renderings generated in the schematic phase of a project should reflect the preliminary nature of the presentation. This means that renderings created for schematic design presentations often hint at the color, finish, and design details of a project. Renderings created for a final design development presentation may be far more refined to allow for communication of details and actual material finishes (Figure C-20). Some designers prefer that renderings retain a sketchlike quality so as to reflect the conceptual nature of the project. Others use only highly detailed, realistic renderings in order to fully communicate project design and to eliminate guesswork by the client.

Regardless of the level of finish, most renderings require that a color and value study be completed prior to the final rendering. To create a color and value study, take a copy of the perspective line drawing and mark the values, shadows, and highlights that will be rendered in each area. Colors must be fully tested on the study prior to beginning the final rendering (see Figures C-21a and C-21b).

Minimally colored perspectives work well when time is limited, when the actual materials have not been finalized, or when one or two hues are predominant. This method is sometimes referred to as "underrendering," which allows for the introduction of color, yet only hints at actual materials.

Shadows are rendered in color in a variety of ways. Shadows often contain the color of their surface in a very dark value. In addition, the color of the object casting the shadow can be subtly washed into the shadow. Shadows are often created by applying warm gray (for warm colors) or cool gray (for cool colors) marker to the appropriate location prior to the application of colored marker or colored pencil. In very soft colored pencil renderings shadows can be created in pencil in the surface color, in a complementary color, or in gray.

COLOR MOVEMENT is another key aspect of color rendering. Color movement is based on the idea that light and color bounce around in the environment. Capturing the reflection of light and the movement of color makes renderings appear rich and interesting. Objects and surfaces should never be rendered in just one color of marker; instead, they should have additional color washed or dotted into them. For example, a red apple sitting on a wood table will bounce a bit of red onto the table surface, and an adjacent wall may also pick up a dot of red from the apple. Because green is the complement of red, a bit of green can be washed into the apple and dotted onto the table as well (see Figures C-19 and C-20).

A simplified method of creating color movement requires that when a color is used on a surface, that same color is washed or stippled into a minimum of two additional surface locations. Incorporating movement of color is a bit strange at first, but it is a useful rendering trick. Objects sitting very close to one another actually wash each other with color, and this color movement must also be considered in rendering.

Along with color movement, renderings require COLOR VARIATION. A hue such as green should be rendered with variations of that hue, not with one layer of forest green marker. Of course, creating value contrast does to some extent create value variation. However, hues should be varied to communicate the actual inherent variation of color found in many materials. Wood floors, for example, have variety owing to graining patterns and actual variations in hue from board to board. Plants have leaves with a range of hues and values; new leaves appear bright and fresh, older leaves become yellow or brown. This type of natural variation in hue must be communicated in renderings. This means that it is not advisable to use any single color of marker for any natural surface—it always looks unnatural.

Color variation can be used to create a focal point in a drawing as well. The focal point of a drawing may contain richly rendered colors. As the surfaces recede from the focal point, they can fade away. This technique creates a lively rendering; it also highlights important points and requires less rendering time.

Interior perspective renderings are complex and vary greatly in technique. It is important to note that there is no single way to render any particular material or setting. The way items are rendered must reflect design intent. For this reason rendering requires the use of extensive reference material. A clip file (or reference file) with hundreds of images of figures, surfaces, materials, plants, and entourage elements is fundamental. It is by examining images that one can render them in a manner appropriate to the project. Professional illustrators keep vast reference archives containing everything from gardening catalogs to plumbing supply catalogs. Sometimes appropriate images can be enlarged and photocopied to reveal value and shadow relationships.

TECHNIQUES AND TIPS

The actual marker strokes used in color rendering interior perspectives should follow the form of an object or be applied with diagonal or curved strokes, indicating highlights and shadows. It is often best to apply marker strokes vertically for walls and floors.

Unsuccessful marker renderings most often suffer from inappropriate use of color and poor marker application. Marker color should not be overpowering; for the most part, it should be subdued and enriched by colored pencil and color movement. Many colored markers are far too intense to be used on large areas of renderings without blending, manipulation, or "tuning up" with pencil or pastel.

Colored pencil and ink can be used to create profile lines and define edges on marker renderings. White gouache and dry pastels can tone down marker color and create highlights and glints. These are applied over the desired layers of marker.

Highly detailed colored perspectives are not used in every design project, but they are used when the project and client can benefit from them. Highly detailed color renderings are often created by professional illustrators. However, the tools and techniques used by illustrators and designers can also be employed by students in the creation of in-process design renderings. These renderings can be used throughout the design process as communication tools. Figures C-23a and C-23b are renderings of the project shown in Figure 5-15b, created during the design process. Figures C-24, C-25, C-26, C-27, and C-28 are student renderings created for various design presentations.

5-15b

Figure 5-16
Computer enhanced elevation.
Software: Adobe Illustrator
by Cory Sherman

As with all presentation methods, rendering and color rendering can be used to explore and communicate. Increasingly, computers are used in rendering to create two-dimensional images and multimedia presentations. A range of rendering and illustration software is employed in the creation of digital images. Figure 5-16 is a fairly simple computer-enhanced elevation. The most realistic computer-generated renderings employ multiple software applications, allowing for sophisticated color, material, and lighting rendition. Figures C-29, C-30, C-31, C-32, C-33, C-34, and C-35 are various examples of computer-generated images.

REFERENCES

Drpic, Ivo. *Sketching and Rendering Interior Space.* New York: Whitney Library of Design, 1988.

Forseth, Kevin and David Vaughn. *Graphics for Architecture.* New York: John Wiley & Sons, 1980.

Green, Gary. *Creating Textures in Colored Pencil.* Cincinnati, OH; North Light Books, 1996.

Hanks, Kurt and Larry Belliston. *Rapid Viz.* Los Altos, CA: William Kaufman Inc. 1980.

Linn, Mike. *Architectural Rendering Techniques, A Color Reference.* New York: John Wiley & Sons, 1985.

McGarry, Richard and Greg Madsen. *Marker Magic, The Rendering Problem Solver for Designers.* New York: John Wiley & Sons, 1993.

Porter, Tom. *Architectural Drawing.* New York: John Wiley & Sons, 1990.

C h a p t e r **6**

Scale Models

INTRODUCTION TO SCALE MODELS

The use of three-dimensional scale models allows designers to study the volume of a given space. Unlike drawings and graphics, which exist on a two-dimensional surface, models reveal the three-dimensional qualities of form. Scale models provide designers with the opportunity to study and review, comprehensively, the elements of a design.

Scale models vary widely in terms of finish, refinement, and time spent in construction. Generally, the level of refinement of a model reflects the stage of the design process in which it is constructed. This means that in the preliminary stages of design, models are often quickly constructed and reflect the preliminary nature of the design; these are referred to as STUDY MODELS or WORKING MODELS. As a project proceeds into design development, models often become more refined and detailed. Those models used as a means of presenting a finalized, fully developed design are often very refined and painstakingly crafted and are commonly referred to as PRESENTATION MODELS or FINISHED MODELS.

Most study models present simplified or abstracted versions of finishes, materials, and colors, yet all elements must be presented in accurate scale. Presentation models also often depict design elements in a simplified manner, with all elements accurately scaled. On some occasions finished models are constructed for design presentations with all materials, colors, and finishes depicted accurately. These highly accurate models are most often constructed by professional model makers. Many architecture and design firms have full-time model makers on staff, and other firms hire model-making consultants as required. These professionals employ a wide variety of materials, techniques, and equipment—ranging from band saws to laser cutters—in the construction of beautiful scale models.

The construction of any model must begin with deciding on its purpose. If the purpose is study and refinement of an in-progress design, a study model is constructed. If the model's purpose is to present a fully developed design to a client, a presentation model is constructed. Furthermore, in constructing a presentation model, thought should be given to the nature of the design presented as well as the presentation audience. For example, if the model is meant to communicate the spatial relationships or functional aspects of a space, the model maker should simplify and abstract the finishes so that they are not the focus of the model.

Projects that are publicly funded often require presentation models to gain public approval, and projects funded by investors may also require presentation models. In these cases, the audience must be considered carefully and the model must work to clearly communicate the design. Models meant for a general audience may require very accurate, realistic depiction of finishes and are often made by professionals.

Models are highly useful as a means of study for students of design. Many design students are more comfortable designing spaces by drawing plans and elevations and avoid constructing scale models. The problem here is that most students have trouble visualizing the totality of a space when they limit their work to two-dimensional drawings. Without a doubt, the best way to come to know the totality of any space is to build a scale model; it is also a wonderful way for design students to improve design visualization skills.

Constructing quick study models of in-process designs allows students to "see" a space very early in the design process. Study models are often constructed rapidly, using inexpensive, readily available materials. Given the way interior spaces are planned, interior study models are often constructed by attaching vertical elements directly to a drafted floor plan. A basic understanding of materials and construction techniques will allow design students to construct helpful study models.

MATERIALS AND TOOLS

PAPERBOARDS

Various types of paperboards available in art supply stores are used in scale model building. For the most part, paper products are inexpensive, lightweight, and easy to cut. Figure 6-1 illustrates a range of paperboards used in model building.

Figure 6-1

Various paperboards used in model making.
1. Foam board (white)
2. Foam board (black)
3. Foam board (colored)
4. Corrugated board (commonly called cardboard)
5. Ripple wrap
6. Chipboard
7. Mat board (with black core)
8. Museum board (white)
9. Illustration board
10. Mounting board (black)
11. Bristol board
Photograph by Bill Wikrent.

FOAM BOARD (also called foam core) is a type of paperboard, consisting of polystyrene foam (or Styrofoam™) sandwiched between two sheets of paper. Foam core comes in a variety of thicknesses, is often sold in 3/16-inch or 1/8-inch thicknesses, and is readily available in bleached white paper with a white center. Also available are black foam core, consisting of black cover paper and a black foam center, and foam core that is primarily white with one colored top layer.

White foam board is commonly used for study models and works well because the thickness of foam core relates well to standard scaled wall thicknesses. Most often foam board is left unpainted to serve as a neutral or abstract presentation of materials. Sometimes designers cap foam core edges with another paper such as bristol board or museum board to cover the exposed Styrofoam, which gives a more refined appearance.

Foam board is easily cut with snap-off cutters or X-acto™ knives. When cutting foam board, it is important to use very sharp blades and to cut in a minimum of three steps. The first cut is made through the top layer of paper, the second cut should go through the middle layer of Styrofoam, and the last cut must cut cleanly through the bottom paper layer (Figure 6-2).

Do not try to cut through foam board in less than these three steps; otherwise, the effort will result in jagged edges. Only very sharp blades should be used, as dull blades produce poor results. When required, the paper can be peeled from away from the foam center and the foam can be cut, sanded, or scored. This allows for the creation of angles, curves, and other complex shapes (Figures 6-3, 6-4, and 6-5).

White glue works well in joining foam board. When required, straight pins are used to hold joints together while the glue dries. In complex models, angled weights and clamps may be used. Spray adhesive and double-sided tape also work with foam board. As stated, most often foam core is left unpainted, creating attractive, simple study models. If painting is desired, paint must be carefully tested on a scrap of foam core, as some paints dissolve the foam.

Foam board is also used as a mounting surface for materials presentations, drawings, and renderings. Although it works well in this application, foam core can warp, depending on weather conditions, paper surfaces, and adhesives used.

GATOR BOARD™ (also called gator foam) is similar to foam core, in that it consists of foam sandwiched between layers of paper. This material is very sturdy and is difficult to cut. Gator Board is best cut on a band saw. As with foam board, the outer layers of Gator Board can be peeled away, allowing the inner foam to be cut and sanded. White glue works well in Gator Board scale models, as do spray adhesives and double-sided tape.

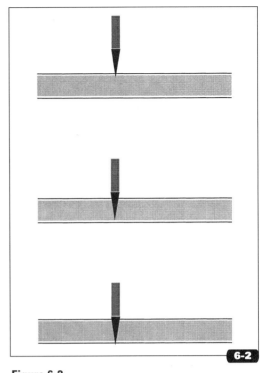

Figure 6-2
Cutting paperboard.
When cutting paperboard, three separate cuts should be made. First the top paper surface is cut, then the middle surface, and, finally, the bottom paper surface is cut.

Figure 6-3
When using foam board, a 45-degree angle is cut by first peeling away a portion of the top surface that matches the thickness of the board. Then the inner material and bottom layer of paper are cut at 45 degrees. Two sheets cut this way can be joined together to form a 90-degree angle. Photograph by Bill Wikrent.

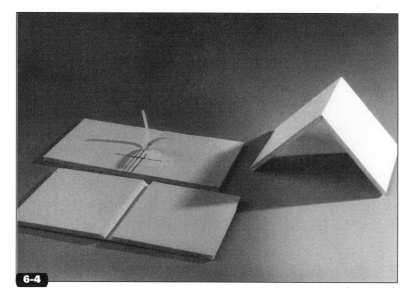

Figure 6-4

When using foam board, a 90-degree angle can be formed by removing a portion of the top paper surface that is twice the thickness of the foam board. Each side of the foam core is then cut away at a 45-degree angle with the backing paper left in place. The board is then folded to create a 90-degree angle with a continuous paper surface. Photograph by Bill Wikrent.

Gator Board is available in bleached white as well as black; it also works well in presentation boards, especially for heavy items. Gator Board is used occasionally as a mounting surface for drawings and renderings because it does not warp as easily as foam board.

CORRUGATED BOARD (commonly called cardboard) is generally brown in color, inexpensive, and used in constructing study models. Corrugated board consists of heavy corrugated paper covered with outer layers of heavy brown paper. The outer layers of corrugated board may be peeled away to reveal the corrugated paper center. This corrugated center can then be used to indicate texture. Corrugated board works well in quick study models because it is widely available, inexpensive, and can be cut easily. Although it is easy to cut, this material requires the three-cut method discussed earlier in regard to foam core. White glue works well with corrugated board, as do spray adhesives and double-sided tape.

Another kind of paper that is currently available looks like the corrugated center portions of corrugated board; this is often referred to as RIPPLE WRAP. Ripple wrap is available in a wide range of colors and is used in the creation of presentation boards, notebook covers, and portfolio covers, as well as in model making.

CHIPBOARD looks like the outer layer of cardboard (corrugated board). It is extremely inexpensive and is used on quick study models. Chipboard cuts easily with a cutter or an X-acto blade and can be fastened with white glue, spray adhesive, or double-sided tape. MAT BOARD is paperboard with a colored top surface. It is available with a white or black paper center. Mat board is sometimes used to add color and details to models, and on some occasions models are constructed completely of mat board. MUSEUM BOARD generally has a high rag content and is white or off-white throughout. Museum board is used to create pristine study and presentation models because of its attractive appearance.

ILLUSTRATION BOARD most often has a white or buff-colored surface, a high rag content, and can be used for model making. Black MOUNTING BOARD is thin and easy to cut, as is BRISTOL BOARD (or bristol paper), which is often white. All of these paperboards require three cuts through the paper surfaces to produce a clean-looking cut area.

Chipboard, mat board, museum board, black mounting board, and bristol board are easily cut, lightweight, easy to glue, and are often used in model making. Because they are thinner than foam core, they work in smaller scale models. In large scale models these thinner paper boards are laminated (layered together using glue or double-sided tape) or used in conjunction with additional paperboard, wood, or plastic.

WOOD

Wood is often used in scale model building. Because it is more costly and time-consuming to work with, it is not used as often as paper products in quick study models. It is, however, widely used in models during the design development of a project and for final presentations. Because of its warmth and natural beauty, wood is often treated very simply and abstractly in models. It may be sanded, stained, or sealed but is rarely painted or heavily embellished. It is useful to use wood in models where wood is to be a major interior finish.

A variety of wood products useful in model building are available in hobby stores. Particular wood species offer certain advantages. Figure 6.6 illustrates wood products used in models.

BALSA WOOD is a light and porous wood that can be cut with a blade or knife (or a saw on larger pieces) and requires no power tools for cutting. Because it is easy to carve, balsa wood is used for toy making, crafts, and scale model building. Balsa wood is readily available in blocks, strips, sheets, and veneers (very thin sheets) in a wide range of sizes. Because of its fibrous nature, this wood may appear rough even after sanding. Although balsa wood can be cut easily, it can be difficult to cut evenly because of the structure of the wood.

BASSWOOD is an attractive, smooth, light-colored hardwood that is very popular for model building. It has only slight graining patterns, giving it a neutral appearance useful in models. In addition, basswood is relatively easy to cut and work with. Unlike balsa wood, basswood can be sanded smooth if handled carefully. Basswood is sold at many hobby stores, especially those that specialize in railroad models or miniature houses. It is available in blocks, sheets, veneers, strips, dowels, cut with siding patterns, and in scaled, ornamental moldings. Thin sheets and strips of basswood can be cut with a sharp X-acto blade or a utility knife, whereas thicker slabs and blocks require hand saws or power tools.

Other hardwood species such as walnut, mahogany, cherry, and teak, available in sheets, veneers, and blocks, are used in models. Because these woods have distinct patterns of graining and coloration, they are often used to accent basswood models. In constructing highly detailed models, it is helpful to use the actual wood species that is proposed for a particular design. Often hard-to-find wood veneers are available at local specialty woodworking shops.

White glue is often used in the construction of wood models. It is best to apply white glue sparingly, as this provides better adhesion and a neat appearance. Because white glue requires time to dry, items should be weighted, clamped, or otherwise held in place as the glue dries. In some cases instant glue is used on wood models. Many expert model makers rely on slower versions of instant glue such as Slow Jet™ or Slo-Zap™, especially when gluing small or complex items.

PLASTICS AND FOAM

Plastics are used by professional model builders and by industrial designers for scale models, mock-ups, and working prototypes. Styrene, polystyrene, and Balsa Foam™ are some of the most popular

Figure 6-5
Create curves with paperboard by first scoring the material (leaving the backing paper intact) and then securing the board in place with glue. Photograph by Bill Wikrent.

Figure 6-6
Wood is often used in presentation models.
1. Balsa wood (strips and blocks)
2. Cherry
3. Walnut
4. Basswood (strips, veneer, and
   scaled moldings)
   Photograph by Bill Wikrent.

6-6

plastics for use in model and prototype construction. Figure 6-7 illustrates types of plastics used in model building

STYRENE sheets, strips, rods, and I-beams are available at hobby
shops in a range of sizes with a white finish. A variety of grooved and
scored sheet styrene is available in patterns that resemble tiles, siding,
and other finish materials. Sheet styrene is cut by scoring with a sharp
blade and then snapping along the scored area. Sheet styrene is best
glued with specialized plastic cement that creates a fast and strong bond
that actually fuses the joint.

STYRENE FOAM insulation board is lightweight and readily available at lumberyards and home improvement stores. This material is
most often sold in in blue, pink, and gray and in a range of thicknesses. Sheets of styrene foam can be glued together (or laminated) to form
the desired width and depth. The best means of cutting styrene foam is
a hot wire cutter. Nonrepositionable spray adhesive works well as a glue
in layering foam. Styrene foam presents a problem in terms of toxici-
ty and does not accept paint well. It is best used unpainted in study
models or as an abstraction of material form.

BALSA FOAM is a tan-colored, nontoxic, phenolic polymer resin
foam that is easier to work with than standard styrene foam. Balsa Foam
can be readily cut with simple hand tools (knife blades, cutters, and
saws) and is easily glued with low-melt hot glue or spray adhesive. If
required, Balsa Foam can be painted with acrylic or enamel paints. It is

available through model railroad shops and catalogs geared to industrial designers.

Sintra™ is a polyvinyl chloride product used in point-of-purchase displays and signage construction. This material is increasingly used by model makers. Much like sheet styrene, thin sheets of Sintra are cut by scoring and breaking along the score. Sintra is available in varying thicknesses and colors and can sometimes be painted with acrylic paints over appropriate primers (this works only for models; displays require different paints). Paint may be applied by brush, airbrush, or spray can.

ADHESIVES AND TOOLS

Model making requires tremendous patience in measuring, cutting, gluing, and attaching. Certain tools and adhesive products can make the job of model construction easier. However, the most important tools of all are patience and allowing the proper amount of time. Figure 6.8 illustrates popular modeling tools and adhesives.

WHITE GLUE, such as Elmer's Glue-All™, is used a great deal in model construction. It works well on paper, foam core, Gator Board, and wood. White glue forms an excellent bond; however, it takes some time to dry. This means that the items being glued must be held in place by clamps, weights, or hands. Generally, white glue should be applied in thin layers to create neat, tight joints. White glue applied in thick layers does not hold well and looks terrible.

Figure 6-7

Plastics are often used in study models and for portions of presentation models.

1. Styrene foam (cut into blocks)
2. Balsa Foam™ (cut into cylinders)
3. Sintra™ (colored)
4. Sintra (white)
5. Styrene (strips, rods, grooved sheets, plain sheets)

Photograph by Bill Wikrent.

Figure 6-8

Model building tools and adhesives.

1. White glue
2. Slow instant glue
3. Glue accelerator
4. Glue stick
5. Rubber cement
6. Double-sided tape
7. Transfer tape
8. Masking tape
9. Painters tape (removable)
10. Spray adhesive
11. Sandpaper
12. Small file
13. Tack Cloth (for removing debris after sanding)
14. Small, heavy angle plate (used as a weight)
15. Large paper clips
16. Small clamps
17. Straight pins
18. Utility knife
19. Snap-off cutter
20. Excel™ (or X-acto) knife
21. Metal builder's square
22. Cork-backed metal ruler
23. Steel straightedge with knob
24. Cutting pad

Photograph by Bill Wikrent.

RUBBER CEMENT is an excellent adhesive for bonding paper and light fabrics to paperboard in models or materials presentations. When using rubber cement, be sure to apply the cement lightly to both surfaces, let it dry a bit and become tacky, and then attach the two surfaces. This type of application allows for repositioning of the cement. Rubber cement is flammable and can produce toxic vapors.

INSTANT GLUES have the advantage of drying quickly and the disadvantage of drying so fast that mistakes are made. Many model builders use slow versions of instant glue such as Slow Jet or Slo-Zap. These slower quick glues allow for objects to be set in place and repositioned. Once the items are in place, an accelerator such as Zip Kicker™ or Zap Kicker™ is sprayed on the joint and the glue dries instantly.

The use of slow glues and accelerators is necessary in constructing detailed and refined models with complex elements. These instant glues work well on wood but do not work on styrene. They are highly toxic and flammable and should be used only according to manufacturer's instructions in extremely well ventilated work areas.

DOUBLE-SIDED TAPE (including transfer tape), masking tape, and painters tape all work well in model construction. Double-sided tape is excellent for attaching and layering sheets of paper, foam core, and wood veneers. It works better than spray adhesive, which can cause warping of dissimilar surfaces.

TRANSFER TAPE is sold in rolls; it is sticky on both sides yet contains no sheet of plastic to hold the adhesive. It can be applied by hand or with a transfer tape gun (sold in some art supply stores). Transfer tape works well for layering paper and thin veneers and causes little telegraphing of the tape through the veneer. This tape is excellent for attaching paper to foam core or mat board and generally causes no warping.

MASKING and PAINTERS TAPE work for masking off areas and bonding items together. Long-Mask™, or painters tape looks similar to masking tape but is blue in color. The advantage to painters tape is that it is easily removable and leaves no residue even after several days. This allows the model maker to leave the tape in place while paints and glues dry, without having to remove the tape too soon.

SPRAY ADHESIVE is used like spray paint. The adhesive is sprayed from a can onto the appropriate surfaces. Some types of spray adhesives adhere permanently, and others allow for repositioning. Spray adhesives are very popular with design students. In model making, spray adhesive is most commonly used in attaching copies of plans and elevations onto foam core for use in study models. This is a fast and effective method of study model construction.

Although spray adhesive is quick, it is important to note that paper applied with spray mount to foam board will eventually wrinkle or bubble if applied to large surface areas. It is wise to use repositionable spray mount in model construction and materials presentations. However, almost all spray adhesives can cause wrinkling and warping of paper and foam board if left for any period of time. One trick to removing a spray adhesive is to use a hair dryer to warm it before attempting removal. The overspray from spray adhesives can be messy, and these adhesives generate fumes and are flammable.

STUDIO TAC™ is an alternative to spray adhesives. This is a double-sided adhesive sheet sold in a range of sizes. Studio Tac is peeled away from a backing paper and applied to the object for mounting; it is then peeled away from another backing surface and mounted. Studio Tac works best in adhering lightweight items such as paper and paperboard. It produces no overspray or fumes.

HOT GLUE guns are electric guns that heat and dispense hot (or very warm) glue. Glue guns hold sticks of glue that melt and are pushed through a nozzle; they are popular with many hobbyists and have some applications for models. However, hot glue is messy, hard to control, and, in many cases, does not produce a strong bond. Hot glue is used more often in the construction of quick study models than in refined presentation models. Hot glue can cause gaps to form in joints and can fail in completed models.

Generally, hot glue is more useful in adhering materials to presentation boards than in assembling scale models. Glue guns range in size and in temperature. High-temperature glues work best for fabric, some plastics, glass, wood, and ceramic. Lower-temperature glues are often used for Styrofoam, paper, and more delicate materials.

X-acto knives and blades are commonly used in model building, as are snap-off cutters and utility knives. A wide range of blades are available for use with X-acto (or similar brand) knives. The range of blades provides for specialized cutting uses, although the classic fine-point blade (# 11) is most useful in cutting paperboards. Cutters with snap-off blades also work well because they allow for easy changing of blades.

The key to using all types of knives and blades is to work with a *sharp* blade and make many cuts through the paperboard or wood. Foam board, mat board, museum board, bristol board, and cardboard all require at least three cuts through their surfaces. The three-cut method is the only way to achieve neat and tidy cuts, and it requires absolutely sharp blades.

A specially designed polyvinyl cutting pad is very useful for cutting all types of materials. Most cutting pads have a grid pattern that allows for alignment. These pads protect table surfaces, provide a nice, measured cutting surface, and seem to make blades last longer.

A cork-backed metal straightedge is an excellent cutting edge for model making. In addition, steel straightedges are available with knob holders; these protect fingers from cutting accidents. Plastic rulers and triangles are not to be used for cutting edges as they are easily damaged and do not work well.

Professional model makers sometimes use heavy angled plates, as well as clamps, to hold pieces together while glue sets up. These are necessary for detailed and complex models and are not used as often by students for study models.

Bob Feyereisen, a busy professional model builder, has stated that the six most important items for model making are a steel triangle with knob holder (to protect fingers), a polyvinyl cutting pad with a horizontal wood edge attached (for use in conjunction with the tri-

6-9

Figure 6-9

Figure 6-9
Bob Feyereisen's top tools for
students.
1. Transfer tape
2. Painters tape (blue)
3. Elmers white glue
4. X-acto
5. Steel straightedge with knob
   (Bob recommends a metal
   triangle with knob.)
6. Cutting board fitted
   with wood to use with
   straightedge or triangle
Photograph by Bill Wikrent.

angle), an X-acto knife, white glue, double-stick tape, and Long-Mask tape (Figure 6-9).

CONSTRUCTION OF STUDY MODELS

As stated, all types of model building require patience and time. The first step in model construction is careful consideration of the purpose of the model. If the purpose is for the designer(s) to study spatial relationships and proportions, a very quick study model can be constructed. Quick study models are most often constructed of chipboard, cardboard (corrugated board), mat board, museum board, or foam board.

As a project is refined, a more refined model may be used to study design details and finishes; in this case the study model must be more detailed and may be shown to a client for approval. Refined study models are often constructed of illustration board, mat board, museum board, foam core, or wood (or some combination of these materials). Refined study models may also include plastic or acrylic, for indication of glazed surfaces.

A common method of constructing a quick study model involves gluing orthographic drawings to chipboard, corrugated board, or foam core. This is done by first gluing the floor plan in place on the model making material, such as foam board. The interior elevations are then glued onto foam core, chipboard, or corrugated board, attached to the plan, and glued in place. It is advantageous to use scaled human figures in study models. These can be drawn by hand and glued to foam core.

When gluing orthographic drawings, it is important to consider the eventual thickness of the walls and to plan accordingly. Figures 6-10a, 6-10b, and 6-10c illustrate the steps in constructing this type of study model. Figure 6-11 depicts a model constructed similarly, with the exception that the orthographic drawings are attached to a building section, creating a sectional model.

The materials selected for this type of study model must relate to the scale of the model. For example, a model constructed in 1/8″ scale requires exterior walls that scale to roughly 1/16″; in this case thin museum board or mat board would be an appropriate choice (Figure 6-12).

Some designers prefer pristine, monochromatic models. In such cases simply gluing an elevation onto paperboard is not appropriate. A model like this requires that measurements be taken from orthographic drawings and transferred to paperboard. The paperboard is cut to the correct dimensions, and the model is then glued in place. Figure 6-13 illustrates a study model constructed by transferring dimensions instead of attaching elevations.

For the most part, it is best to avoid using manufactured doll-house products in study models. Such items tend to be too busy and distracting. Instead, abstracting materials to simple forms is useful and less distracting. However, some milled wood items such as paneling and interior moldings can be used to good effect in study models. Figures 6-14a and 6-14b are simple models with abstracted finishes.

6-10a   6-10b

Figure 6-10a
Quick study models are often constructed by first attaching the floor plan to foam board, then attaching the elevations to foam board. It is best to plan ahead and leave extra room at either side of the appropriate elevations in order to attach the adjacent walls.
Photograph by Bill Wikrent.

Figure 6-10b
The walls are glued into place on the plan. Notice that the extra room at each side of the first wall elevation allows for gluing and joining the adjacent wall.
Photograph by Bill Wikrent.

Figure 6-10c
An overview of the steps of
construction.
Photograph by Bill Wikrent.

6-10c

FLIP-UP MODELS

Simple square or rectilinear spaces can be illustrated with flip-up models. These models use floor plans and interior elevations that are rendered and glued onto a paperboard surface. The elevations are then attached to the plan with a single strip of tape placed on both back surfaces. The tape serves as a hinge and allows the elevations to flip up into place. The elevations can be taped into place as needed for study and review. Figures 6-15, 6-16 and 6-17 illustrate flip-up models.

Figure 6-11
A sectional model (a section
fragment model) of the
Unite d'Habitation, designed
by Le Corbusier. This model
was part of a demonstration
of quick and efficient model
building for students.
Model by Thomas Oliphant.
Photograph by Bill Wikrent.

6-11

Figure 6-12
A model built to study wall heights, constructed of museum board mounted on black foam board.
Design by Courtney Nystuen.
Model by Leanne Larson and the author.
Photograph by Bill Wikrent.

Figure 6-13
Study model constructed of illustration board.
Model by Eric Zeimet.
Photograph by Bill Wikrent.

6-14a

6-14b

Figure 6-14a
A vignette model built to study wall finishes, constructed of foam board, rendered matboard, basswood veneer, and basswood dollhouse moldings. Photograph by Bill Wikrent.

Figure 6-14b
A vignette model built to study wall finishes and design, constructed of mat board, rendered mat board, ripple wrap (metallic finish), and basswood veneer. Photograph by Bill Wikrent.

The use of flip-up models is a way to use drawing skills as an aid in model making, and these models can be stored flat for inclusion in a portfolio. The limitation of flip-up models is that they work only for very simple floor plans and are less realistic spatially than standard models.

SCALE MODELS IN PROFESSIONAL PRACTICE

Some design firms use scale models a great deal, and others use them rarely. Highly refined presentation models take hours to build and are very costly. For this reason some designers do not use them. However, many designers have a commitment to study projects fully during the design process, and this requires the use of scale models. It also requires that design contracts include the costs of model building.

Larger firms often have a fully equipped model shop where a range of models are constructed for study and presentation. In many firms, designers build only study models and professional model builders are hired to build presentation models.

Firms that use models as a fundamental part of the design process often construct many models in the course of a project. This means that a series of models are constructed that reflect the levels of refinement of the design. Figures 6-18, 6-19, 6-20, 6-21, and 6-22 illustrate a series of models built for one design project. Figures C-36 and C-37 are color images from this project.

On very large design projects, such as hotels and entertainment facilities, full-scale mock-ups may be constructed. It is not unusual for large hotel projects to employ full-size room mock-ups for viewing by

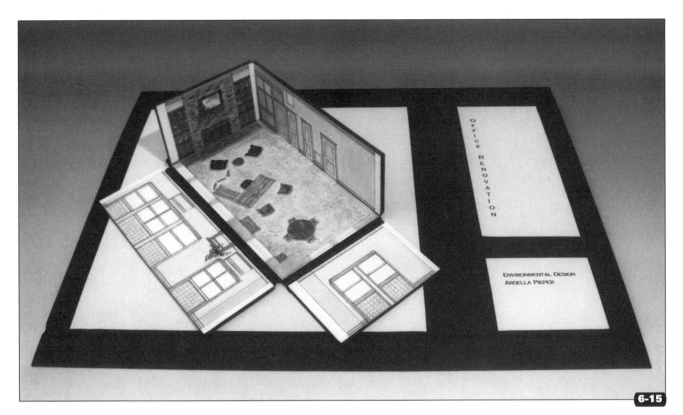

Figure 6-15
A rendered flip-up model.
Constructed of rendered bond
paper on black foam board.
Model by Ardella Pieper.
Photograph by Bill Wikrent.

Figure 6-16
A rendered flip-up model.
Constructed of rendered paper
(with computer graphics) on
foam board.
Model by Rachel L. Mayer.
Photograph by Bill Wikrent.

Figure 6-17
A rendered flip-up model.
Constructed of rendered paper
on foam board.
Model by Rachel L. Mayer.
Photograph by Bill Wikrent.

investors or owners. Unusual design details may also require full-scale mock-ups as a means of study prior to construction.

Industrial designers create a number of study models throughout the design process. These models are made of a variety of materials, ranging from foam board to styrene and Balsa Foam (Figures 6-23 and 6-24). In an ongoing process of refinement, industrial designers often create many models for each project, ending with absolutely accurate presentation models that can be mistaken for the real thing.

In the specialized process of designing furniture, it is necessary to construct many models and mock-ups. Furniture study models are often constructed of corrugated board, chipboard, foam board, or styrene. As a design becomes refined, it is often necessary to move to large-scale mock-ups or prototypes as a means of studying form as well as working out construction issues. Prototypes are required to perform as the actual products will, and thus are often constructed of materials very similar to the actual final product (Figures 6-25 and 6-26).

Figure 6-18
An overhead view of a large study model built for a professional project, constructed of bond paper, foam board, plastic, teak veneer, metal screen, and fabric.
Design and model by Meyer, Scherer, & Rockcastle, Ltd.
Photograph by Bill Wikrent.

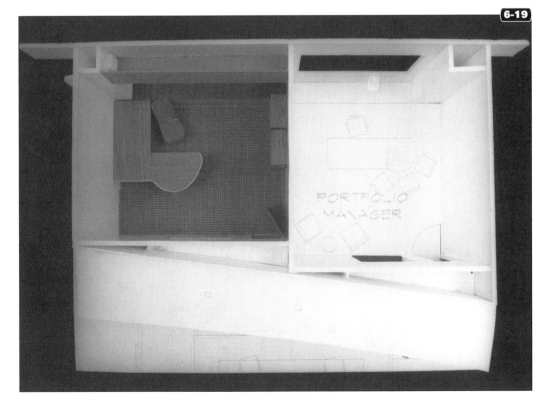

Figure 6-19
An overhead view of a smaller study model built for a professional project (also shown in Figure 6-18), constructed of bond paper, foam board, plastic, basswood, teak veneer, and fabric.
Design and model by Meyer, Scherer, & Rockcastle, Ltd.
Photograph by Bill Wikrent.

Figure 6-20
Side view of the study model
shown in Figure 6.19,
constructed of bond paper,
foamboard, plastic, basswood,
teak veneer, and fabric.
Design and model by Meyer,
Scherer, & Rockcastle, Ltd.
Photograph by Bill Wikrent.

Figure 6-21
Furniture models for the project
featured in Figures
6-18, 6-19, and 6-20, con-
structed of assorted wood.
Design and model by Meyer,
Scherer, & Rockcastle, Ltd.
Photograph by Bill Wikrent.

Figure 6-22
Furniture model for the project
featured in Figures 6-18, 6-
19, and 6-21, constructed of
assorted wood and metal.
Design and model by Meyer,
Scherer, & Rockcastle, Ltd.
Photograph by Bill Wikrent.

Figure 6-23
Study model of a videophone,
constructed of foam board.
Design and model by
Evan Sparks.
Photograph by Bill Wikrent.

Figure 6-24
Study model of a portable
stereo, constructed of
Balsa Foam.
Design and model by
Jill Holterhaus.
Photograph by Bill Wikrent.

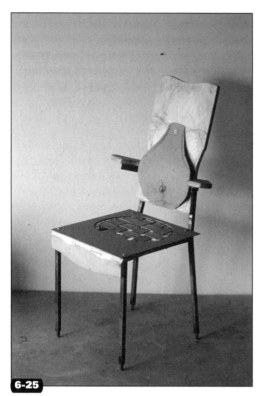

6-25

Figure 6-25
Chair prototype constructed of
wood and steel.
Designed and made by
Thomas Oliphant.
Photograph by Kathy Fogerty.

Figure 6-26
Chair prototype (on right) shown
with actual finished
chair (on left).
Designed and made by
Thomas Oliphant.
Photograph by Kathy Fogerty.

6-26

REFERENCE

Shimizu, Yoshiharu. *Models and Prototypes: Clay, Plaster,
Styrofoam, Paper.* Tokyo: Graphic-sha Publishing
Company, 1991.

Chapter 7

Presenting Materials and Finishes

INTRODUCTION TO
MATERIALS PRESENTATIONS

Most professional interior design projects involve study, review, and refinement of interior architectural finishes and materials, as well as furnishings, fixtures, and equipment. Finish materials, furnishings, and fixtures must be studied individually and must also be viewed as parts of a whole. All of these items must be evaluated in terms of life safety issues and performance as well as from an aesthetic standpoint. This chapter focuses only on the presentation of these items and does not cover the important issues of life safety, performance, and specification.

A formal materials presentation is not of particular importance to the individual designer as an aid in the design process. It is most common for designers to gather a variety of samples and make preliminary decisions without "pinning anything down." Most designers can work from large samples kept loose (unmounted) while in the preliminary stages of a design (Figure 7-1). It is necessary to create formal presentations for clients, end users, or investors only when selections have been determined or narrowed down. Large projects, or those with many team members, may in rare cases, require a materials presentation as a communication and design aid. These cases are the exceptions, not the rule.

Early in the space-planning process many designers begin to consider architectural finishes and materials. After careful study, preliminary selection of finishes, materials, and furnishings can be made. These preliminary selections are presented to the client or end user in a way that reflects the preliminary nature of the selections.

Often preliminary selections of materials are presented at the same time as preliminary plans, elevations, perspective or axonometric drawings, and, perhaps, study models. All of the elements used in a particular presentation must be consistent graphically and work best if they contain unifying elements. For example, if it is used in a preliminary presentation, a materials board may incorporate the graphics found in the title block of drawings. Or perhaps the format of a materials board can be consistent with the format used to present renderings. In many cases, materials boards are keyed graphically to floor plans and serve as an aid in understanding elements of the design presented.

Some designers prefer to keep the preliminary materials presentation casual, with all elements remaining loose and unmounted. Providing loose items allows the audience for the presentation to touch and easily examine the samples. Keeping things loose also allows the client to understand clearly the preliminary nature of the selection and imparts a sense that there is plenty of room for decision making.

7-1

Many designers mount preliminary selections on presentation boards so that the client or end user gets a sense that decisions have been made and are being communicated. Another method of preliminary presentation calls for pinning samples down on a formal board with push-pins, so that they can easily be removed for examination by the client.

As a project moves forward, it is important that materials presentations clearly reflect the given stages of the design. Many designers create a materials presentation as part of the final visual presentation, which takes place at the end of design development phase of a project. Large and complex projects often require several materials presentations, which occur at key points in the design development process. Some projects, however, may require no formal materials presentation during the entire design process.

One extremely successful residential designer never mounts materials onto boards for any project. He keeps all samples loose and arranges them on a worktable for his clients' review. Several designers interviewed prefer to drape fabrics on full-size furniture samples and keep all finishes unmounted for client approval.

Clearly, there is variation in the manner in which finalized selections of materials, furnishings, and finishes are presented to clients. Many designers pride themselves on consistent, well-crafted materials presentations, whereas others prefer to keep samples loose and informal. Most firms have standards for the way presentation boards are presented. These standards include preferred board size, color, graphics, and methods for attaching samples, as well as the level of formality conveyed in the presentations.

The presentation standards employed by an individual firm allow presentations to distinctly reflect the concerns and focus of the firm and at the same time clearly convey the selections for a particular project. Final presentations often include drawings, renderings, models, and materials boards, all of which must appear visually cohesive and logical.

On some projects, all of the elements for a final presentation, including materials boards, must be packed for travel. This means that all necessary items are included and everything of importance must be packed and organized for the designer's arrival in a strange city. Organizing a final presentation for travel can take weeks of preparation. There are large projects that include more than 50 materials boards that must be packed for travel and presentation to large audiences. Presentations of this sort must be organized in a clear and logical fashion, leaving no margin for error.

The variation in practice and presentation of interior design projects requires that design students develop a range of skills in preparing materials presentations. Fortunately, internships often provide an excellent opportunity for students to become involved in creating all types of design presentations, including materials presentations, thus allowing the students to see particular office standards as they relate to these presentations.

Although there is great diversity as to formality of presentation and office graphic standards, there are numerous factors common to all materials presentations. These have to do with legibility, organization, graphic cohesion, quality of craftsmanship, techniques, and tools, and appropriateness. All design students can benefit from a clear understanding of these factors in developing visual skills and creating meaningful presentations.

MATERIALS AND MEDIA

Many of the materials used in presentation boards are discussed in previous chapters. Information on types of paper and drawing tools can be found in Chapter 1; additional information on paper and rendering media is found in Chapter 5. For descriptions of paperboards, adhesives, and cutting tools, refer to Chapter 6.

Most materials presentations require sturdy backing materials, most often a type of paperboard. Foam board is often used in such presentations because it is sturdy, yet lightweight and easy to work with. Samples, titles, and notes can be applied directly to the top paper surface of the foam core. White foam board is commonly used, although some favor black foam board for more dramatic presentations. Figures C-38, C-39, C-40, C-41, C-42, and C-43 depict attractive, well-organized, professional presentations mounted directly on white foam core board.

In some presentations foam board is covered with mat board, illustration board, bond paper, or Canson™ paper. Samples and titles are then mounted to the top paper surface. When thinner papers such as bond paper or Canson paper are used, the entire paper surface can

X   Y   Z
Design Group
123 Billable Hwy
La Jolla CA 92100

7-2

Twin Tall Towers
Lobby Renovation

be laid out with titles and notes and printed on a large-format photocopying machine; samples are then added to the appropriate locations (Figure 7-2).

Smaller or lightweight materials may be mounted on lighter-weight boards such as mat board, illustration board, or museum board. However, lighter boards can appear flimsy and will not support heavy materials such as tile or stone samples. Mat board and museum board are sometimes cut with windows; then samples are mounted behind the windows just as artwork is matted (for further information, see the discussion later in this chapter under "Window Matting").

Materials presented in professional practice are often large and quite heavy. Full-size ceramic tile, glass, and stone samples are particularly heavy. For this reason Gator Board or wood panels are used as a mounting surface in some professional presentations. Large pieces of Gator Board can be used with minimal warping, as can wood panels. Gator Board and wood also allow for the mounting of very heavy samples (see Figures C-55, C-56, C-57, and C-58).

Professional practice also requires very large-scale sample mock-ups to be provided on some jobs. For example, it is not uncommon to create 3′ x 3′ ceramic tile sample mock-ups for large projects such as shopping malls and airports. These large-scale samples are often provided by the appropriate subcontractors on a project. However, in some cases they are created by design firms.

Nontraditional projects often require nontraditional materials presentations. One designer uses galvanized sheet metal, with magnets holding samples in place, for nontraditional presentations. A recent presentation made use of chain link fencing panels as a mounting surface. Clearly, appropriateness is important in selecting nontraditional presentation modes. Figures 7-3, 7-4, 7-5, and C-44 are nontraditional materials presentations.

A variety of adhesives are used to mount samples, and a variety of mounting techniques are employed in materials presentations (see "Basic Techniques" later in this chapter).

7-3

Figure 7-3
This board employs bond paper mounted to foam board, with the materials arranged in a nontraditional manner. The bond paper contains a scanned image of the design parti.
Photograph by Bill Wikrent.

ORGANIZATION AND COMPOSITION

In materials presentations there is great variety in the placement of samples and materials, yet designers generally agree on the importance of planning the arrangement of presentation graphics.

Stylistically, boards may vary greatly. However, regardless of style or method of sample organization, some basic principles of graphic design should be employed in laying out presentation boards. For example, the use of a grid can do wonders for any presentation (see Chapter 6). Traditionally, presentations with multiple boards should have a consistent compositional orientation: all boards should be formatted vertically, all horizontally, all square, and so forth.

Regardless of the style of presentation, materials boards should have actual or implied borders. A border may be drawn, printed, or created with graphic tape (plastic or vinyl tape is available in a range of thicknesses and colors), or the border area may be left blank with no samples or titles placed within a given area. Figure 7-6 shows thumbnail sketches of border arrangements.

7-4

Figure 7-4
This board employs bond paper mounted to foam board, with the materials arranged in a nontraditional manner. The bond paper contains a scanned and manipulated image of the floor plan.
Photograph by Bill Wikrent.

There are distinct and diverse opinions regarding the organization of samples for presentations (Figure 7-7). One school of thought calls for materials to be laid out in relation to the actual physical location of materials. This means that all flooring is placed at the bottom of the arrangement, furnishings are placed above flooring, wall finishes are placed above flooring, window treatments and ceiling materials are placed at the top of the arrangement.

It is also common for designers to place items that relate to one another in close proximity on the presentation board. For example, a picture of a chair will be mounted adjacent to the wood finish sample and the upholstery sample for that chair. This method is useful for clients who are not accustomed to viewing presentation boards, such as corporate officers or home owners.

Another school of thought calls for materials to be placed according to their visual impact within the composition. For example, on a project with hundreds of yards of rubber floor tile and very little carpeting, the presentation may show large samples of rubber flooring and smaller samples of carpeting.

Some designers place samples of exactly the same size on the board and lay them out in equally spaced horizontal bands. Others place important items in the center of the presentation and spin additional samples out from the center. A few designers use the floor

Figure 7-6

Boards look best with some type of border.

1. Borders may be implied (dashed lines), with no items displayed beyond the implied borders.
2. Borders may be defined with a window mat.
3. Borders can be drawn onto the board surface or applied with graphic tape.
4. Borders may be defined with a sheet of colored paper mounted on foam board.

Figure 7-7

Board organization.

1. Materials applied in relation to their location in the environment: flooring at the bottom, walls above flooring, ceiling materials at top of board.
2. Materials applied in relation to proximity or physical contact; for example, flooring adjacent to related furnishings and finishes.
3. Materials placed according to their visual impact on the composition; for example, large areas of flooring represented by large samples.
4. Materials placed in relation to a graphic element or design parti; in this example, the materials form a collage relating to the floor plan.

plan of a given space as an abstract diagram for laying out the materials on a presentation board.

There is a bit of controversy in regard to whether samples should physically touch one another on presentation boards. For years designers were trained to lay out samples with blank spaces (negative space) between samples. In current practice this is no longer considered important by some designers, who think that items that will touch in reality should touch on boards.

Many designers place black or white cloth tape on the edges of materials boards. The tape can hide the several layers of material that would otherwise be exposed at the edge and creates a neat, clean look. A black taped edge creates a distinct border, whereas a white taped edge is less visually dominant. Certain designers find a taped edge unnecessary if the boards have been cut cleanly.

On occasion, clients require that materials boards be framed and placed behind glass. This is most common when presentations will be viewed by investors or hung in the sales or leasing office of a developer of commercial real estate. In these cases the particular needs of the audience must be considered in the titling and layout of the boards.

TITLES, KEYS, AND LEGENDS

It is imperative that all materials presentations clearly communicate the items selected. This means that samples must be titled, referenced, or keyed. There are two basic systems of referencing samples and images on presentation boards. One method requires that all items be titled or labeled directly on the front of the board, adjacent or very close to the appropriate sample. Another method allows for samples to be keyed and referenced with a legend on the front or back of the board or on an accompanying document. Designers and firms most often have office standards that call for some form of one of these methods. Figure 7-8 shows thumbnails of some methods of titling and keying boards.

There are many board titling methods. Some designers prefer labels to be kept simple; for example, a carpet sample may simply be labeled "Carpet—Master Bedroom" or "Carpet." Other designers prefer that actual specifications be included in the title; for example, the carpet would be labeled "Carpet—Master Bedroom, Wool Berber, 42 oz., Helios Carpet Mills." Some designers prefer simple titles on the front of the board with full specifications keyed to the back of the board, or keyed to a floor plan.

Systems for keying or referencing samples vary as well. Some designers prefer a letter or number code that relates to the type of sample used. For example, carpet may be listed as "C-1," wallcovering as "WC-1," and both are then fully referenced on the back of the board. Other designers prefer a simple numbering or lettering system starting with "1" or "A," running through all of the samples and referenced on the back.

Some designers prefer a system that employs no titles or codes on the front of the presentations. Instead, a duplicate image of the

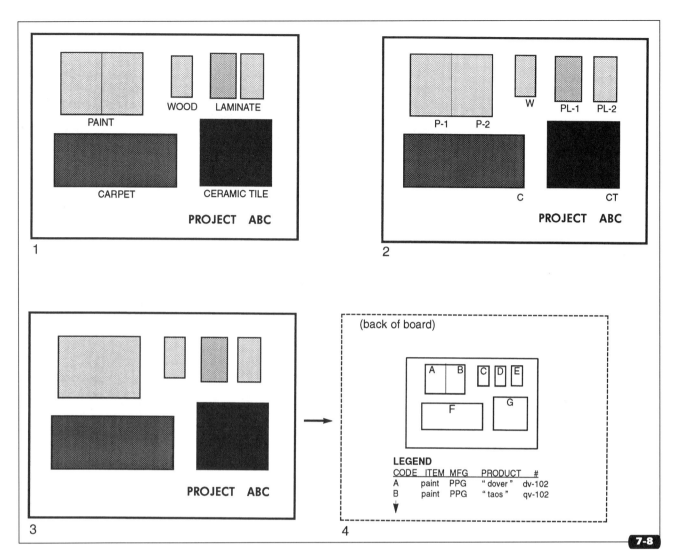

board appears on the back with samples specified or referenced. It is also common to key materials to related floor plans or elevations and use the orthographic drawings as part of the reference system. For example, a materials board may have a code "C-1" for a particular carpet; the locations for the carpet are then shown on an accompanying floor plan.

There are many ways to create the actual titles used on boards. The simplest titles are created by hand lettering. In some cases lettering is drawn directly on the top surface of the presentation board. A more professional look is created by drawing letters on paper, mounting the paper on paperboard, and applying that on top of the presentation board surface. In either case, drawing vertical and horizontal guidelines and using a straightedge for vertical portions of letters is imperative. Press-on type, available in a variety of type styles, may be used in a manner similar to hand-drawn lettering.

Many designers and students use machines that print type onto plastic tape, such as Kroy™ or Merlin™ machines, in creating titles for presentations. After the machine expels the printed tape, a plastic

Figure 7-8
Board titles.
1. Materials may be titled directly on the board.
2. Materials may be titled using a code system, with a legend or key placed on the back of the board.
3. This example employs no titles on the face of board; instead, a coding system and legend are used on the back of the board.
4. Borders may be defined with a sheet of colored paper mounted on foam board.

Figure 7-9
In wrapping fabric samples, first allow an appropriate amount of material for wrapping. Then pull the ends firmly in place and secure with glue or tape. Adding a piece of paperboard to the back of the wrapped sample allows for easy mounting and gluing.
Photograph by Bill Wikrent.

backing is peeled away and the tape is mounted to the board surface or raised mat board title plates, much as in hand lettering. It is imperative that the tape lettering is neatly cut and applied to boards with the use of guidelines.

Appliqué film (sticky back) is commonly used in titling boards and drawings for presentation. Almost any graphics may be photocopied onto sticky back. The film is then cut to size and the backing surface removed, allowing the graphic to be applied to any paper surface. Sticky back works well in creating neat titles and unusual graphics, such as logos for boards and drawings. Sticky back can be found at most commercial photocopier supply stores and is available in a range of finishes from matte to glossy. Designers often select a matte finish for titling materials boards. It is imperative that appliqué film is measured and cut neatly (an X-acto works well). In applying film to any surface, vertical and horizontal guidelines are required. For more information on appliqué films, see Chapter 1.

Most computer word processing software will allow for printing a range of type styles. This means that students and designers with computers can create beautiful titles by simple computer generation of the appropriate words. The titles may then be mounted directly, or first applied to paperboard and then mounted (with the use of guidelines).

Titles, borders, and notes can be laid out on a large sheet of paper and photocopied on a large-format photocopier (or a standard copier for boards 11-by-17-inches and smaller). The large photocopy is then mounted on paperboard and samples are attached. This method allows titles and logos to be printed on colored papers that accept photocopy toner. The colored paper is then mounted on paperboard, and samples are applied to the colored paper (Figure C-45).

Basic Techniques

Currently, given the time constraints of professional practice, most designers mount or attach samples to the front surface of a presentation board. This method requires samples to be neatly mounted with all edges trimmed or wrapped.

Fabrics are often wrapped around cardboard (or mat board) and taped or glued in place. This treatment produces neat, uniform samples with no unraveled edges. Figure 7-9 illustrates the construction of these samples. The same wrapping method can be used on formal boards for paint samples (Figure 7-10). When it is necessary to save time, fabric samples can be neatly trimmed and placed on mat board, which is then glued to the presentation board. In appropriate circumstances fabric samples may be draped and glued in place (see Figure 7-5).

Pictures or photocopies of furnishings and equipment look best if they are mounted (with double-sided tape, Studio Tac, or spray mount) on mat board, which is then trimmed and mounted directly on

Figure 7-10
Paint samples can be wrapped around a cardboard form and held in place with tape. Photograph by Bill Wikrent.

7-10

Figure 7-11
Photographs look best
mounted on mat paperboard
and then trimmed and glued
onto a board. A paper cutter
makes quick work of trimming.
Photograph by Bill Wikrent.

7-11

the presentation board. Placing these items on mat board allows for them to sit on top of the surface of the presentation board, creating a shadow line and adding a professional finish to the board; it also can prevent warping (Figure 7-11). The fastest method of trimming photos that are mounted on mat board is to use a large paper cutter with a sharp blade. This is quicker than cutting with a utility knife or X-acto. Replacement blades are available for paper cutters, which greatly enhance their performance.

When mounting heavy objects such as tile, stone, or metal panels it is sometimes necessary to score the mounting board surface prior to applying glue. Scoring the surface adds texture to the board and increases the bonding capacity of most glues. This is especially necessary if Canson or another art paper is applied on top of a mounting board. Often, the paper must be cut away to reveal the mounting surface, so objects are glued directly to the backing board. This prevents the sample from pulling the Canson paper from the backing board. A consistent, thin application of white glue can often bond heavy samples to boards. In rare cases, contact cement is used, but because it is toxic and rather unpleasant to work with, it should be used as a last resort.

Especially large or heavy samples may require two layers of foam board to be used as backing. This allows one layer of the foam board to be cut away so that the sample may be recessed into the opening.

Plastic laminates and other samples may have product numbers printed on them. These printed numbers can often be removed with an electric eraser. Bestine™ or another solvent can also be used to remove stubborn printed information.

Designers use a variety of adhesive products in mounting samples and materials. A relatively thin application of white glue works beautifully in adhering lighter and medium-weight samples. However, white glue will cause light papers (tracing paper, vellum, bond) to wrinkle. In mounting these papers, double-sided tape, rubber cement, or spray-on adhesive (for small areas) can work well. Studio Tac works very well in adhering paper and light samples to board surfaces.

Hot glue can work wonders in creating materials presentations if it is used on light- to medium-weight items with large, flat surface areas. Heavier samples will not bond well with hot glue. A fairly thin, consistent application works best. Big globs of glue are not only messy, they do not create enough surface area of glue for a good bond. It is imperative that care is taken to prevent the hot glue from spilling onto the presentation board surface.

Sometimes it is necessary to remove an item that has been glued permanently in place. Hand-held hair dryers may work to warm and loosen a variety of adhesives, such as spray-on adhesive, StudioTac, hot glue, rubber cement, and sticky back. A warm setting is usually best, as a hot setting may cause melting or warping.

There are some technical issues to consider in mounting a presentation. It is generally a mistake to use spray adhesive to mount large bond or print paper drawings to foam board or mat board. Boards mounted in this fashion will wrinkle or warp—or both. It is far superior to use Studio Tac or rubber cement to mount these lightweight drawings. In some cases drawings may be mounted on Canson or other art papers, which creates a thinner presentation format that can be inserted into a portfolio.

Some designers prefer to use large black clips (available at office supply stores) to attach drawings to foam board or precut plywood sheets (the exact size of the drawing's surface). This allows drawings to be easily removed and replaced with revised drawings.

WINDOW MATTING

Some designers and educators prefer formal boards with samples placed behind neatly cut window mats. Clearly, window mats create very tidy and clean presentation boards. However, cutting a window for each sample is time-consuming. Because time and budgets are constant factors in design practice, some designers have forsaken this presentation method and others use individual window mats only for very formal presentations or those that will eventually hang in sales rooms or developers' offices. Some design firms continue to employ window-matted presentation boards.

Window matting requires that the board be designed and laid out with all of the samples and items in place. Window locations are drawn on the surface of the mat board, and the windows are cut in the marked locations. If a beveled edge is required, I recommend using a commercially available mat cutter. Mat cutters range in price from about $30 to more than $1,000. Mat cutters generally provide a housing for a cutting blade that slides along a metal straightedge, providing a beautiful beveled or straight cut. Most mat cutters create a beveled edge by making cuts from the back of the mat board surface; this can become quite confusing when many windows are to be cut.

Figure 7-12
When cutting window mats by hand, it helps to precut the corners.

Figure 7-13
Window mats often allow items to project from the windows.
Photographs by Bill Wikrent.

Figure 7-14
The nature of some materials requires items to be recessed beneath window mats.

Figure 7-15
Interior view of matted flat artwork. The drawing is taped to the back of the window, and the backing board is hinged at the top with tape. To preserve artwork, only archival materials should come in contact with the artwork.

7-12

7-13

7-14

7-15

When cutting windows by hand, it is imperative to use a very sharp blade. It is also important that the cutting blade is used to make a minimum of three cuts: one through the top, one through the middle, and one through the bottom paper surface. Making three cuts will create clean, sharp edges. It is also a good idea to use a fresh blade for each window. To avoid overshooting the corners of windows with the blade, try to precut corners (Figure 7-12). A nail file can be used to smooth ragged cuts when necessary.

In window matting, samples are attached to the backing board, then the front board with windows is placed on top (Figure 7-13). In some cases, the mat board lies on top of the samples to create a presentation where the samples are recessed behind the windows (Figure 7-14). It is common for boards with window mats to have taped edges that conceal the many layers of material involved. In presentations employing window mats it is also common to include window-matted drawings. In these cases, a window is cut in a board and that board is hinged (using tape) to a backing board. The flat drawing is then taped over the back of the window (Figure 7-15), or attached to the backing board. Archival mat board, backing board, and hinge tape are used for matting drawings that should be preserved.

DESIGNING THE TOTAL PRESENTATION

Many of the materials and methods discussed in this chapter are employed in mounting drawings, renderings, models, and other elements used in visual presentations. When multiple elements are combined for a visual presentation, all of the elements used must be consistent graphically and must contain unifying elements. This sounds easy, but is typically rather complex. For example, a presentation may include sheets of orthographic drawings or construction documents, renderings, models, and materials boards. Creating unity among such varied formats can be problematic.

The key is to seek a unifying element(s) that will hold the presentation together visually and conceptually. Project graphics, including title blocks, logos, and/or conceptual diagrams may be employed as unifying elements. For instance, the graphics found in the title block on a sheet of orthographic drawings may be used on materials boards and mounted renderings to unify the presentation. In some cases, the actual format of the boards is used as a unifying element. For example, all of the two-dimensional elements of a presentation can be mounted on boards with consistent horizontal bands at the bottom, in a consistent color.

Very formal materials presentations employing window-matted materials may require that renderings are window matted and titled similarly to create unity and consistency. Certainly, there are no hard-and-fast rules in bringing together the many visual aids used in design presentations. However, consistency, clarity, legibility, and craftsmanship are worthy goals. In all cases it is important to carefully consider the presentation audience. An audience familiar with design drawings will require far fewer visual aids than an audience unfamiliar with viewing floor plans and elevations. Moreover, an unfamiliar audience requires far clearer titling and greater graphic consistency than a group of design professionals.

The foregoing considerations point to the need for design presentations to be *designed*. Students must see unity of presentation as a *design problem*, rather than approach it as an afterthought. In designing and developing a presentation, it is worthwhile to follow the steps of the design process. The presentation should be analyzed, a list of criteria created, and research regarding the audience and available materials undertaken. Synthesis is achieved by the creation of thumbnail drawings and design sketches. The design of the presentation must be evaluated, and only then should the presentation be created.

In analyzing design presentations, it is important first to consider the stage of the design process that is to be communicated. Preliminary presentations are quite different from final design development presentations. Analysis must include the relative sizes of elements, the number of components presented, and the various formats to be employed. The size of the audience and the layout of the room used for the presentation influence the relative size and format of the presentation. Time, as well as budgetary constraints, must be considered.

Once the important issues are analyzed, several sketches can be made of possible presentation formats, and these should be reviewed and evaluated. Possible presentation formats include renderings and materials formally mounted on boards. On some occasions drawings, renderings, sketches, and materials are left unmounted and are simply pinned up in the design firm's conference room (or in some appropriate viewing area), and the client is invited to view the work. In these instances full-size samples of furnishings and equipment may be placed in the viewing area as well. Figures C-45, C-46, and C-47 are examples of student presentations. Case studies highlighting methods of visual presentation used in two professional design projects are illustrated in Figures C-48 to C-68.

REFERENCES

Leach, Sid Delmar. *Techniques of Interior Design Rendering and Presentation*. New York: Architectural Record Books, 1978.

Tate, Allen. *The Making of Interiors*. New York: Harper & Row, 1987.

Chapter 8

Portfolios and Resumes

The mere word *portfolio* can strike fear in the heart of a soon-to-be design graduate. This is because in representing a student's body of work, the portfolio is often the key to getting an excellent entry-level job or internship. And, often, the portfolio becomes symbolic of a student's fears about graduation and employment.

Yes, portfolios can be scary business. They require planning and organization, an expenditure of money, excellent design skills, and a huge amount of effort. Working on your portfolio also signifies that the next step is interviewing, followed by working. This is the goal of many individuals pursuing an education in design. Therefore, working on a portfolio is a commitment to working in design. And, of course, anyone who will hire you without looking at your work is probably not really hiring you to do design.

Creating a portfolio along with a resume, cover letter, and other related items is a necessary step in moving forward as a designer. This is true whether one is searching for an internship, an entry-level job, or (after years of experience) a new job within the design community. The graphic design of one's portfolio, resume, and cover letter must be appropriate to the intended audience. The audience for these materials is most often a design director, managing designer, or human resources director of a firm or corporation. These professionals are busy people who will be reviewing a great deal of information. As a result, economy and organization are key factors in the design of one's employment-generating tools. A basic understanding of the principles of graphic design and general hiring practices can help in creating employment-seeking materials. Some of those principles and concepts are covered in this chapter.

Although some basics are covered here, it is most useful for interior designers and design students to enroll in an introductory graphic design course (more advanced courses are also highly beneficial). Graphic design is a fascinating discipline with a rich history and vast application in the practice of interior design.

GRAPHIC DESIGN COMPONENTS

GRIDS

Good graphic design allows for good communication. Organization and composition lead to clear communication and are important principles of graphic design. For years graphic designers have employed grids as a means of composing and organizing information. Grids provide the framework for the design of any page or two-dimensional surface. Writing in

Figure 8-1
Grids provide the framework
for page design. These are
examples of simple
multicolumn grids and
columns divided into blocks.

8-1

Grids, André Jute (1996) states, "The primary purpose of the grid is to create order out of chaos." He goes on to say, "of all the tools available to help the designer to present a concept in a thoroughly professional manner, none is more powerful than the grid."

Grids offer structure and aid in the organization of data, allowing the reader to easily locate and comprehend information. In addition, grids are very helpful for individuals with little experience in graphic design and page layout. Components of a grid include the actual page size, the margins at the four edges of the page, and the printed area. The printed area is often divided into columns, further dividing the grid structure.

In many areas of graphic design, such as book and magazine design, margins are set according to printing and publication constraints. In resume and portfolio design, however, margins are set rather arbitrarily, based on individual preference. Margins may be equal and uniform or may be asymmetrical, focusing attention on a particular portion of the page. With the margins established, the total print area is defined and columns can be created within the print area. Columns are useful because most people prefer to read short lines of text rather than long lines. Simple grids employ a limited number of columns to carry data. Some occasions call for many columns and further division within columns (usually into blocks). Regardless of the number or width of columns, it is essential that spaces between columns are left blank for ease of reading and clarity of communication. Figure 8.1 illustrates some simple grids.

Thumbnail sketches are required in laying out the elements of a grid. Thumbnails may be drawn by hand or quickly generated by computer. When drawing thumbnails by hand, it is best to work in scale. This means that the thumbnail sketches of an 8 1/2-by-11-inch resume should be drawn in a workable scale.

Grid thumbnails are easily constructed with the use of appropriate computer software such as PageMaker™ and QuarkXPress™. Margins and columns are quickly indicated, allowing the designer to immediately evaluate the layout. In creating hand-drawn or computer-generated grids, it is important to experiment with a range of options. It is also essential to estimate the amount of text required for the document, with important headings or areas of text identified, as one creates thumbnails.

TYPE

According to André Jute (1996), the main purpose of the grid is to organize various typefaces and integrate type and illustrations of varying format and origin. This means that type and illustrations become part of the grid and are significant elements of composition. Understanding basic information about typography is essential for successful graphic design.

Typefaces can be divided into two main categories for purposes of classification: serif and sans serif (Figure 8-2). Serif typefaces have main strokes that end in cross strokes or accents. Sans serif typefaces do not have these cross strokes or accents. Serif typefaces are thought to work best for long passages of text, in that the serif leads the eye across the page. Sans serif typefaces are considered highly legible for a word or group of words that stands alone—such as a headline. Within the two classifications there are many varying typefaces. For example, Avant Garde, Gill Sans, and Helvetica are sans serif typefaces. Garamond, Bodoni, and Palatino are serif typefaces.

Most word processing or page design programs allow for the creation of a number of style choices within a typeface. Underline, *Italics*, **Bold**, ALL CAPS, SMALL CAPS, Shadow, Outline, and Strike Thru are generally available. Very often these styles are overused by those without graphic design experience. Overusing underline, bold, outline, or shadow style can destroy consistency and legibility. To add emphasis within lines of text, it is often best to use the italic style in place of bold or underline. Headings, headlines, and subtitles may benefit from the use of bold style.

Word processing and page design programs also allow for the size of type to be altered instantly. Text is easiest to read when set at 9, 10, 11, or 12 points. Most text used in resumes and business correspondence is set at 10, 11, or 12 points. Titles for portfolio elements are generally larger. The size of type selected affects column width. In general practice, column width is limited to fewer than 65 characters. Therefore, when small-sized type is used, columns are generally narrow.

André Jute (1996) sets forth a useful rule of thumb regarding type selection: a designer should remain limited to "sixteen fonts as follows: two typefaces, in two sizes, in two weights, in two styles." It is important to note that Jute is referring to an entire unit of design, such as a book or magazine; clearly, a resume or brochure should employ

Figure 8-2
Examples of serif and sans serif type.

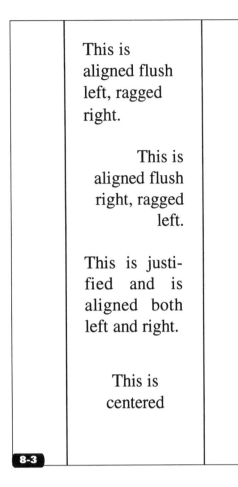

This is
aligned flush
left, ragged
right.

This is
aligned flush
right, ragged
left.

This is justi-
fied and is
aligned both
left and right.

This is
centered

Figure 8-3
Examples of alignment.

fewer fonts. In graphic design, restraint will consistently produce the best results for beginners.

The alignment of type in a column has an influence on the composition of the page and the legibility of the document. Alignment refers to the way type is aligned in columns. Word processing and page design software allow for a range of alignment. Left-aligned (flush left) aligns type to the left column margin. Right-aligned aligns type to the right column margin. Center alignment centers text in the column. Justified alignment creates type that is aligned to both the right and left margins (see Figure 8-3).

Left-aligned text is considered very readable and is the standard setting (default) for most word processing programs. Center-aligned text can appear quite formal; however, centering large blocks of text can diminish legibility. Right-aligned text is somewhat unusual, but in some cases it is useful. Although justified text creates blocks of type with crisp margins, it can become heavy compositionally.

Proper spacing between letters, words, and paragraphs is impor-tant. Most word processing and page design programs automatically establish spacing between characters. However, in certain cases there appears to be too much space between characters and the spacing requires adjustment. Adjusting the space between pairs of letters is called kerning. The amount of space between lines of type is called leading. Leading can be adjusted in most word processing or page design programs. For purposes of legibility, it is common to increase leading as the line length increases.

The preceding discussions of grids and typography are related to the design of resumes, personal identity systems, and business correspondence. Although grids are very useful in the design and layout of portfolios, most portfolios do not require extensive text. Therefore, portfolios will be discussed separately in this chapter.

Most individuals seeking design-related jobs should create the following: a resume, cover letters or letters of application, a thank-you letter, an acceptance letter, and a refusal letter. In addition, most recent graduates find that a promotional mailer sample portfolio can help in getting one's foot in the door for interviews. Most firms receive cover letters and resumes constantly, and it is often the graphic strength of resumes or promotional mailers that gives potential employers a glimpse of what sets special applicants apart from the crowd.

THE RESUME

In *Your First Resume* (1992), Ron Fry defines a resume as "a written document that attempts to communicate what you can do for an employer—by informing him what you have *already* done—and motivate him to meet you. However, content alone cannot do that job, presentation is almost equally important."

The resume is an essential tool in finding work in design; it is a means of illustrating one's strengths and opening doors to interviews. With the cover letter and the appropriate samples of work, the resume is an introduction to potential employers. This means your resume must be well considered and professional.

Most individuals responsible for hiring new employees are very busy and must wade through large numbers of resumes and cover letters. For this reason, a resume must clearly illustrate one's attributes in an eye-catching manner. The resume must be brief and legible, and at the same time must elevate one above other applicants.

Designers' resumes are different, on the whole, from those of many other business professionals. We do creative work, and because of this our resumes may be presented in a creative manner. In fact, many of those hiring design professionals look for creative (yet concise and legible) resumes. Burdette Bostwick states, in *Resume Writing* (1990), that creative resumes do not follow a formal pattern or standard format. Burdette goes on to describe the necessity of including only relevant, condensed information in creative resumes. In designing and writing a creative resume one must meet all of the requirements of a traditional resume, yet do so in a creative manner.

Where I teach, we often have successful, professional designers discuss resumes with our senior students. I must say that the students are always amazed that the visiting professionals never agree about resume and portfolio styles and formats. Typically, professionals involved in facilities management or office planning and furniture dealerships are looking for more traditional, restrained resume design. Yet designers engaged in retail, hospitality, or exhibition design are looking for extremely creative, nontraditional resume designs.

The disagreement among design professionals points to a key in resume writing. It is necessary to analyze carefully your own personality, strengths, weaknesses, and employment objectives prior to writing and designing your resume. It is only after you figure out who you are, what you are comfortable with, and what your objectives are that you can create a resume that reflects these issues. The creative resume must reflect you and illustrate who you are.

If you are comfortable with a simple, straightforward resume, that is what you must use. If, on the other hand, you are most comfortable with a dynamic or nontraditional resume, you must undertake to create one. These differing resume styles will clearly appeal to different employers and will set you on your way to making the appropriate employment connection.

One caveat about the creative resume: Do not go overboard with poorly refined designs or an unstructured, ill-conceived resume and use the excuse of "creativity" to get away with it. Resumes must necessarily be professional looking, legible, and work within standard business practices.

There are some basic guidelines that should be considered in designing creative resumes. The use of a grid is highly beneficial for all resumes, and designers should employ some form of grid to provide graphic structure. Generally, employers will find it easiest to deal with a standard letter size, 8 1/2 inches wide by 11 inches long, paper format. Most business correspondence is formatted this way. I have found that resumes printed with a horizontal orientation may become lost in files; using nonstandard paper sizes can present problems, because odd sheets of paper also tend to get lost.

In designing your resume it is important to show restraint in type selection (most often, no more than two different typefaces). It is also important to use restraint in kerning and leading. The paper selected should allow for legibility. Very dark or highly decorative papers may present problems; they can be distracting and can thwart photocopying. It is also best to avoid folds and staples, both of which can be problematic in filing.

Additional guidelines for resumes include careful consideration of the location of your name. Although there are a number of appropriate locations for a name, it is never a good idea to make the name hard to locate. Some employers prefer the name to be placed close to the top margin, for filing purposes. Generally speaking, your name, address, and phone number should be presented in a straightforward manner. Do not confuse creativity with unduly "clever" complications that can frustrate potential employers. Remember, the goals are to attract attention, sell yourself, and allow employers to find you (see Figures 8-4, 8-5, 8-6, 8-7, 8-8, 8-9, 8-10a, 8-10b, and 8-10c).

Creative resumes can be organized in a chronological or functional format. A chronological resume describes work experience in a reverse chronological (last first) order. This type of resume often lists employers' names and the dates the positions were held as a means of organizing information. Short statements relating to activities, duties, and accomplishment are clustered with each position. Chronological resumes are most commonly used by designers with several years of experience in design.

Functional organization groups work experience by function and job duties. Functional resumes highlight related work experience and focus attention on the type of job held, rather than chronology. The organization of a functional resume allows for emphasis on particular experiences. Functional organization is worthwhile for designers who may have held non-design-related jobs but wish to focus attention on design experience. This may be particularly true for recent design graduates who recently held a nondesign job but wish to focus attention on a previously held successful internship.

Burdette Bostwick (1990) has identified a basic resume, appropriate for those entering the job market with little experience. A basic resume focuses attention on career objectives and education and may include extracurricular activities, useful skills such as languages other than English, summer jobs, volunteer work, and interesting hobbies. For those seeking a design-related position, computer skills and specialized class work should be emphasized in the resume and highlighted in the portfolio. In writing all types of resumes it is best to use action words in describing experience.

Many employers look for an employment objective as part of an

Todd Brown
207 Antrim Hall, Menomonie, WI 54751
phone: 715-232-1058   e-mail: brownt@post.uwstout.edu

OBJECTIVE
To gain an entry level design position that will allow me to grow and explore ideas in a creative, professional atmosphere.

EDUCATION
Bachelor of Fine Arts December 1997 graduation. University of Wisconsin-Stout
Graphic Design Major.

Graduate Study August 1993-December 1993. Louisiana State University
Wildlife Biology.

Bachelor of Science December 1992 graduation. University of Wisconsin-Oshkosh
Biology Major, Chemistry Minor.

WORK EXPERIENCE
Graphic Design Intern May 1997-September 1997. Mercury Marine, Fond du Lac, WI
Design of printed materials including business forms, flyers, banners, logos, and manuals requested by marketing and sales personnel. Coordinated print jobs with vendors.

Groundskeeper May 1996-August 1996. Brooke Industries, Fond du Lac, WI
Provided lawn care for clients. Supervised and assisted mentally and physically challenged employees at the work sites.

Bindery Worker January 1994-August 1994 Mercury Marine, Fond du Lac, WI
Produced and packaged publications using guillotine and 3-blade paper cutters, paper drills, folders, wire stitchers, and perfect binders.

Graduate Assistant February 1993-December 1993. Louisiana State University
Coordinated study site activities. Supervised field crews, made daily work schedules, organized data, and implemented study plan with principle investigators.

Civil Engineer's Aid Summers 1988-1989. Mercury Marine, Fond du Lac, WI
Design of printed materials including business forms, flyers, banners, logos, and manuals requested by marketing and sales personnel. Coordinated print jobs with vendors.

SHOWS & AWARDS
Best of Design Show April 1997, 1996, 1995. University of Wisconsin-Stout
Juried, annual show exhibiting top student works in graphic, industrial, and interior design.

Fine Arts Show May 1997. University of Wisconsin-Stout
Juried, annual show exhibiting top student works in the Fine Arts.

Chancellor's Award Fall 1994-1996, Spring 1995, 1997. University of Wisconsin-Stout
Awarded for a semester GPA of 4.0.

Graduate Assistantship August 1993. Louisiana State University
$12,500 per year graduate research assistantship in Wildlife Biology.

ACTIVITIES
Graphic Design Association Active member
University of Wisconsin-Stout student run graphic design association.

AIGA Student Chapter Active member

Stout Typographical Society Fall 1995
Student organization run by the Graphic Communications Management program.

Enjoying the outdoors, physical exercise, collecting music, photography.

REFERENCES
Portfolio and references available upon request.

8-4

Figure 8-4
Graphic design student resume.
Designed by Todd Brown.

David Winkler

21330 Juniper Avenue
Forest Lake, Minnesota 55025
Phone: (612) 232-3537
E-mail: winklerd@post.uwstout.edu

OBJECTIVE I would like a job in graphic design where I will be able to put my knowledge and experience to work. Eventually I would like to be directing a small group of designers.

EDUCATION 1993 - 1997
UNIVERSITY OF WISCONSIN-STOUT
Menomonie, Wisconsin
BFA - Art
Graphic Design
GPA 3.220

AWARDS 1997 Spring/1994 Fall
CHANCELLORS AWARD FOR
ACADEMIC EXCELLENCE
1989 - 1997
NUMEROUS MILITARY AWARDS
1989
EAGLE SCOUT

ACTIVITIES 1995 - present
AIGA / MINNESOTA CHAPTER

EXPERIENCE April 1994 - 1996
DESIGN WORKS OF FOREST LAKE
Sandblasted sign design
Forest Lake, Minnesota
Design Assistant
worked on design concepts,
sign construction, stenciling,
sandblasting quality checks

August 1992 - March 1997
MINNESOTA NATIONAL GUARD
D. Company 1/194 Infantry
Saint Paul, Minnesota
Team leader
supervise and train other soldiers

August 1989 - August 1992
UNITED STATES ARMY
Headquarters, Headquarters Company 3/5 Cavalry
Kirchgoens, Germany
Driver
drove and maintained 1/4
ton truck and a Bradley Infantry
Fighting Vehicle, supervised others,
participated in Operations Desert
Shield/Storm

Separation papers and references
available on request.

Figure 8.5
Graphic design student resume.
Designed by David Winkler.

GREGORY LEE BUNTING

9256 29TH AVENUE NORTH
NEW HOPE, MINNESOTA 55427
612 541 9756
e-mail buntingg@post.uwstout.edu

PROFESSIONAL OBJECTIVE

To obtain an entry level position in the field of graphic design or multimedia production that
would allow me to grow and explore ideas in a creative and professional atmosphere.

EDUCATION

University of Wisconsin, Stout Menomonie, Wisconsin
Bachelor of Fine Arts Degree, Graphic Design Major 1997
North Hennepin Community College Brooklyn Park, Minnesota
Associate of Applied Science Degree, Graphic Design Major 1995

WORK EXPERIENCE

1997	**Leerburg Video Productions** Menomonie, Wisconsin - Graphic Design
1996 - 1997	**Minnetonka Sailing School** Minnetonka, Minnesota - Transportation
1996	**Kinko's Copy Center** Minnetonka, Minnesota - Customer Service
1996	**Rolin Graphics** Golden Valley, Minnesota - Graphic Design

PROFESSIONAL ACHIEVEMENTS

Designed catalog and packaging for Leerburg Video Productions.
Produced published illustrations for Rolin Graphics.
Art work and photos featured in **Under Construction** magazine.
Design Editor for **Under Construction** magazine, 1995-1996.

ACTIVITIES

Active member of the American Institute of Graphic Artists, Minnesota Chapter.
Personal interests include art, music, travel, skiing, skating, camping, hunting and fishing.

References available upon request

8-6

Figure 8-6
Graphic design student resume.
Designed by Greg Bunting.

education

university of wisconsin-stout, menomonie, wi
bfa • **interior design** concentration • 5.98
GPA • 3.7/4.0

winona state university, winona, mn
associate of arts degree
graduated magna cum laude

experience

internship • 5.97-8.97
shea architects, minneapolis, mn
responsible for generation of construction documents created on autocad 13
selected finishes and composed project presentation boards
interacted with clients and reps throughout project design phases

art director • 6.96-8.96
girl scouts of the milwaukee area, milwaukee, wi
planned weekly art activity schedule
created art activities for entire camp
supervised campers during art sessions

lab supervisor • 9.95-5.97
uw-stout interior design lab, menomonie, wi
organized and maintained lab references and materials
implemented efficient organization ideas for lab facility

desk supervisor • 9.95-present
uw-stout antrim/froggatt hall, menomonie, wi
advised hall residents, staff, and guests with questions or concerns
maintained positive customer relations

floral designer • 6.95-9.95
dj campus floral, winona, mn
experimented with a variety of floral mediums
designed floral arrangements

organizations and activities

asid student chapter liaison • 1997-98
asid newsletter chairperson • 1997-98
asid junior representative and publicity committee member • 1996-97
art and design student advisory council member • 1997-98
participated in asid regionals, minneapolis, mn • 1996-97
participated in the asid student chapter career day • 1996-98
participated in the frank ching drawing workshop • 1996

exhibits and honors

work exhibited in best of design shows, uw-stout • 1997,1998
work featured in *interior design visual presentation* by maureen mitton
to be published by john wiley & sons • new york, new york
chancellor's award for academic excellence • 1995-present

computer skills

autocad release 13
photoshop 4.0
illustrator 7.0
freehand 7.0
quark xpress 3.3

references and portfolio

available upon request

a r d e l l a   p i e p e r

school address

436 froggatt hall
menomonie, wi 54751
telephone 715.232.1738
piepera@post.uwstout.edu

permanent address

rural route one, box 139
rushmore, mn 56168
telephone 507.478.4324

Figure 8-7
Interior design student resume.
Designed by Ardella Pieper.

REBECCA A. ZAGLIFA
2208 North Ninth Street
Wausau, Wisconsin 54403
Phone: (715) 849-3024
Fax: (715) 843-5287
E-mail: nbzag@dwave.net

OBJECTIVE   To obtain a position as a Graphic Designer.

EDUCATION   University of Wisconsin-Stout, Menomonie Wisconsin.
Bachelor of Fine Arts degree in Graphic Design
December, 1997

Northcentral Technical College, Wausau Wisconsin.
Associate of Applied Science degree in Architectural & Residential Design
June, 1994

WORK EXPERIENCE   Summer, 1997
Roto-Graphic, Wausau Wisconsin.
Pre-press Production Assistant
Responsibilities included digital and traditional stripping of negatives,
preparing paper and metal plates for print, paste-up digitally and traditionally,
scans, and photographing camera-ready work.

August, 1994 - June, 1995
Pamida Stores, Inc. Menomonie and New Richmond Wisconsin.
Sales Floor Associate
Responsibilities included customer assistance and check-out, stocking
merchandise, and general maintenance of the Hardline Sales areas.

May, 1994 - August, 1994
The Worth Company, Stevens Point Wisconsin.
Assembly and Shipping Department Associate
Responsibilities included assembly, packaging, and preparing merchandise for
shipment to area department stores.

AWARDS & ACTIVITIES   Dec. 1997   UW-Stout cum Laude Graduate.
June, 1997   UW-Stout Chancellor's Award for Academics.
1997-1998   UW-Stout AIGA of Minnesota.
1995-1997   UW-Stout Graphic Design Association.

REFERENCES & PORTFOLIO   Available upon request.

8-8

Figure 8-8
Graphic design student resume.
Designed by Rebecca A. Zaglifa.

JASON
GILMOUR
GRAPHIC DESIGN
PHOTOGRAPHY

618½ 3RD ST. #6   MENOMONIE WI 54751
715.235.2573   GILMOURJ@POST.UWSTOUT.EDU

OBJECTIVE
To utilize my design skills and talent in a creative fashion for a business seeking to aesthetically improve the design quality of its clientele.

EDUCATION
1997
University of Wisconsin-Stout
Bachelor of Fine Arts degree
Graphic Design major
3.4 cumulative GPA

WORK EXPERIENCE
SKYLINE DISPLAYS, INC.
Design Intern [July 1996 to Sept. 1997]
   Worked in marketing and commercial graphics/production department scanning chromes, producing comps, and various in-house and client-based design projects

THE STOUTONIA (weekly campus newspaper)
Staff Photographer [Sept. 1995 to April 1996]
   Photographed 2-3 events per week around campus and rolled and developed film
Photography Editor [April 1996 to Dec. 1997]
   Hired photographers, trained them in photojournalism and darkroom techniques, dispersed photo assignments, critiqued photos, managed darkroom, chose photos to publish, scanned film, color corrected, assisted in layout and design of newspaper, assisted in maintaining of several computers, and wrote music reviews and several editorials

SPORTS STAR PHOTOGRAPHY
Photographer [July 1997 to present]
   Assisted photographers and photographed at youth sports team photo shoots

EXTRA-CURRICULAR
AIGA Minnesota Chapter
   Member [Sept. 1997 to present]
Graphic Design Association (UW-Stout)
   Member [Sept. 1995 to Dec. 1997]
Art & Design computer lab
   Volunteer Monitor [Sept. 1994 to May 1996]
Chi Alpha/Christians in Action
   Member [Sept. 1993 to Sept. 1997]
   President [Oct. 1994 to May 1996]
Power 100 (campus radio station)
   Disc Jockey [Sept. 1993 to May 1995]
Co-ed & league softball
   Utility [May 1993 to present]

PORTFOLIO
& REFERENCES
Available upon request

8-9

Figure 8-9
Graphic design student resume.
Designed by Jason Gilmour.

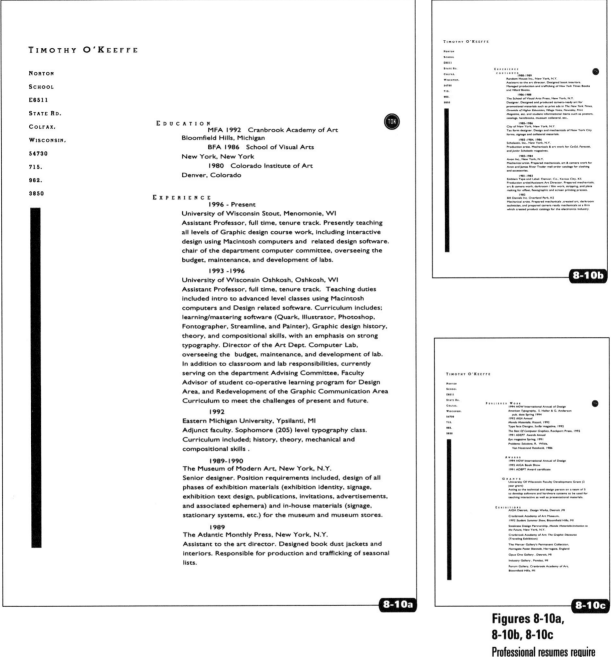

TIMOTHY O'KEEFFE

NORTON
SCHOOL
E6511
STATE RD.
COLFAX,
WISCONSIN,
54730
715.
962.
3850

EDUCATION
MFA 1992 Cranbrook Academy of Art
Bloomfield Hills, Michigan
BFA 1986 School of Visual Arts
New York, New York
1980 Colorado Institute of Art
Denver, Colorado

EXPERIENCE
1996 - Present
University of Wisconsin Stout, Menomonie, WI
Assistant Professor, full time, tenure track. Presently teaching
all levels of Graphic design course work, including interactive
design using Macintosh computers and related design software.
chair of the department computer committee, overseeing the
budget, maintenance, and development of labs.

1993 -1996
University of Wisconsin Oshkosh, Oshkosh, WI
Assistant Professor, full time, tenure track. Teaching duties
included intro to advanced level classes using Macintosh
computers and Design related software. Curriculum includes;
learning/mastering software (Quark, Illustrator, Photoshop,
Fontographer, Streamline, and Painter), Graphic design history,
theory, and compositional skills, with an emphasis on strong
typography. Director of the Art Dept. Computer Lab,
overseeing the budget, maintenance, and development of lab.
In addition to classroom and lab responsibilities, currently
serving on the department Advising Committee, Faculty
Advisor of student co-operative learning program for Design
Area, and Redevelopment of the Graphic Communication Area
Curriculum to meet the challenges of present and future.

1992
Eastern Michigan University, Ypsilanti, MI
Adjunct faculty. Sophomore (205) level typography class.
Curriculum included; history, theory, mechanical and
compositional skills .

1989-1990
The Museum of Modern Art, New York, N.Y.
Senior designer. Position requirements included, design of all
phases of exhibition materials (exhibition identity, signage,
exhibition text design, publications, invitations, advertisements,
and associated ephemera) and in-house materials (signage,
stationary systems, etc.) for the museum and museum stores.

1989
The Atlantic Monthly Press, New York, N.Y.
Assistant to the art director. Designed book dust jackets and
interiors. Responsible for production and trafficking of seasonal
lists.

8-10a

8-10b

8-10c

**Figures 8-10a,
8-10b, 8-10c**
Professional resumes require
careful consideration in
organization and design.
This resume belongs to a
professional graphic designer.
Designed by Timothy O'Keeffe.

entry-level resume. If included, this should be a briefly stated objective for the immediate future—the next two to three years. A well-stated objective can tell an employer a great deal about you and your communication skills. A vague, poorly stated objective can land your resume in the trash. Some employers find objectives trite and tedious. Therefore, if you do not have a genuine objective, it may be best to omit this feature.

Recent graduates should assess the strengths of their programs of study and highlight these educational strengths in their resumes. Course work in construction and construction documents, business, specialized computer software, human factors, universal design, and related fine arts activities should be noted. This does not mean that you should list every course taken. Instead, focus on what made your education extraordinary. Student membership in design organizations and service projects should be included as well. Remember, your resume must set you apart from the competition.

Recent graduates with prior nonrelated education and work experience often employ a combination of the functional and chronological resume formats. This can be done by clustering related activities chronologically. It is exceedingly important that individuals with multiple life experiences seek interesting and appropriate ways to communicate them in resumes. It is also important for those with a few years of design experience to alter the basic resume to clearly communicate experience.

Additional Correspondence

It is customary to send a cover letter with a resume as means of stating your interest in a job. In addition, a thank-you letter, letter of acknowledgment, and letter accepting or declining an offer are useful. One of the best reasons to design an original, creative resume is that you can use the grid (or format), type, font, and any logo on all correspondence used for your job search. A cover letter using design components found in the resume is a very attractive and enticing promotional item. Following up an interview with a similarly designed thank-you card is an excellent idea that says volumes about a designer's skills and professionalism.

There are varying circumstances encountered in applying for a job: a position may be advertised; a job may be communicated by word of mouth. In other cases a resume and cover letter may be sent to a huge number of firms and companies (this is known as broadcasting or generalized mailing). Because there are a range of circumstances, a cover letter must be sent with the resume as a means of introducing yourself, describing your interest in a position, and briefly listing your qualifications.

A successful cover letter generates enough interest for the reader to turn the page and review your resume. In most cases a brief cover letter is best—everyone's time is valuable. Although there are significant variations, most cover letters include an introductory paragraph. This is where you describe your interest in the company, or state that you are answering an ad, or that a mutual acquaintance links you to the employer.

In a generalized mailing it is common to simply introduce yourself, whereas in a letter targeted for a particular position you may lead with why you are interested in working for the particular firm or company.

The cover letter then continues with a partial list of your qualifications (including information about your recent degree or job). The final paragraph should recap, with interest and enthusiasm, the points stated. Be clear and brief; do not waste the reader's time by going over in detail what is covered in your resume. Some applicants find it useful to include a stamped postcard with the resume and cover letter. The postcard can be preprinted with responses such as "We are not hiring at this time," to be mailed back to the applicant.

All forms of business correspondence discussed require accuracy and correct spelling and grammar (do not rely on spell-check alone). By being brief and to the point, you demonstrate business acumen and professionalism. Although a resume can be quite nontraditional and creative, other forms of correspondence should follow standard business conventions. A good book on resume writing and job seeking can be worth the cost.

Employers are often deluged with resumes and cover letters from recent graduates. An excellent resume and cover letter go a long way in getting the door open. However, in some cases more is required. It may be necessary to actually include samples of work with a resume and cover letter. Most often this entails creating a mailer or sample portfolio. (See Figures 8-11a, 8-11b, 8-11c, 8-12a, 8-12b, 8-12c, and 8-12d.)

A sample portfolio is an interesting means of offering a quick look at your work. I have found that recent graduates with well-designed sample portfolios cause quite a stir with employers and are often called for interviews. In designing sample portfolios, careful consideration

Figure 8-11a
Sample portfolio ready
for mailing.
By Jill Stifter.
Photograph by Bill Wikrent.

Figure 8-11b
Sample portfolio as seen
when opened.
By Jill Stifter.
Photograph by Bill Wikrent.

Figure 8-11c
Sample portfolio as seen
with contents fully displayed.
Photographs of special projects
were reduced and mounted on
well-designed project cards; a
resume and a reply card are
included.
By Jill Stifter.
Photograph by Bill Wikrent.

must be given to items for inclusion and the overall cost of mailing. Sample portfolios are expensive, time-consuming, and should be used only for targeted firms or known job openings.

The most inexpensive sample portfolios contain reduced black-and-white copies of design projects and student work. These may be photocopies or images scanned into a computer and used in conjunction with page design software. Reduced color photocopies are also an option for sample portfolios. Graphic designers and product designers use slides extensively in sample portfolios; interior designers use them less often.

Sending samples of work along with a resume and cover letter creates the need for a well-designed package to house the items. When designing a sample package it is important to consider mailing regulations and ease of opening and review. In some cases the package can be designed for return, with postage and return instructions enclosed. However, the party who receives the documents has absolutely no responsibility to return them.

THE PORTFOLIO

Putting together a design portfolio requires the selection of appropriate items for inclusion, the selection of a format (or grid) for the items included, the selection of an actual portfolio case to house the contents, and some practice in presenting a portfolio.

The selection of items is a primary step in creating a portfolio. This requires taking an inventory of all student projects and assignments, as well as items completed during an internship or specialized study. It is important to assess the items honestly and decide which

8-12a

8-12b

8-12c

8-12d

Figure 8-12a
Sample portfolio ready
for mailing.
By Bill Sterna.
Photograph by Bill Wikrent.

Figure 8-12b
Sample portfolio partially
opened.
By Bill Sterna.
Photograph by Bill Wikrent.

Figure 8-12c
Sample portfolio opened to
reveal letter, resume,
and business card.
By Bill Sterna.
Photograph by Bill Wikrent.

Figure 8-12d
Sample portfolio opened to
reveal slides and slide
descriptions.
By Bill Sterna.
Photograph by Bill Wikrent.

Figure 8-13

Portfolios and presentation cases.

1. Zippered presentation case with binder, sheets, and sheet protectors
2. Zippered portfolio for use with individual boards (no binder)
3. Hard-sided portfolio (no binder)
4. Attaché case (individual boards, no binder)
5. Handmade box (individual boards, no binder)
6. Small presentation case with binder, sheets, and sheet protectors (excellent for photographic and smaller images)
7. Inexpensive coated paper or fiber portfolio (no binder)
8. Easel binder with sheets and sheet protectors (usually no larger than 18" x 24")

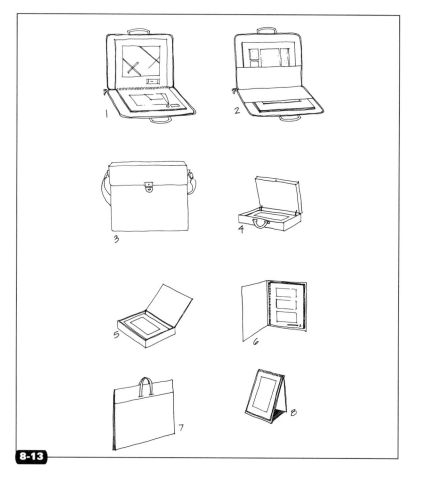

8-13

projects are excellent and ready for inclusion, which items require reworking, and which should be tossed out.

In selecting items, it is essential to include a range of project types. Residential, commercial, small and simple, large, "real," and highly conceptual projects all have a place in a portfolio. It is also useful to include a range of types of presentation. Currently, it is important to include computer aided drafting and design (CADD) pieces and additional computer-generated imagery, as well as construction documents, if possible.

Many soon-to-be-graduates wonder whether all projects should be presented completely consistently, or, instead, whether projects should be treated individually in terms of graphics and format. Unfortunately, there is no hard-and-fast answer to this question. Like resumes, portfolios reflect the tastes and personality of the individual. This means that for some a portfolio that is completely consistent graphically is the only possibility; for others a diverse portfolio with a range of project formats, sizes, and styles is best.

Creating a portfolio that is completely consistent means that all items must be exactly the same size, similar in color, and consistent graphically. This often requires that all projects be redone for inclusion in the portfolio, an expensive and time-consuming proposition. Another drawback is that this type of portfolio presentation does not show projects as they were done for class assignments and therefore may not indicate growth or improvement (see Figure C-47 for an example of a consistent portfolio format).

Portfolios that present projects with a range of graphic styles require some element of unity to tie the projects together. In these portfolios the quality must be consistent, so often a few projects are redone for greater legibility or graphic unity. It is also useful to limit, to some degree, variation in the size of boards and sheets presented, as too much variety in size can be confusing and messy.

Regardless of the consistency of format, all portfolio presentations benefit from elements that add unity and cohesion. The best way to create graphic unity is to use a consistent or similar grid for all projects presented. When this is not possible, a consistent typeface, title block, or logo may be employed. In some cases, perhaps the only possible unifying element is the size of items presented.

Students often ask how many projects to include, and that is difficult to answer. The best way to decide on quantity is to take an inventory of the projects you wish to present, then do a mock-up presentation or run through, and check for time. It is best to limit the presentation to a half hour (for entry-level jobs). Although many interviews go on for longer than an hour, some are cut short and you must make sure all the best work is presented in the time allotted. First interviews often take between a half hour and a full hour. When setting up an interview, it is reasonable to ask how much time will be allowed. Knowledge about the interview time can allow you to edit items in the portfolio.

Questions often arise as to sequence or organization of projects. Much like resumes, portfolios may be organized chronologically or functionally. Generally, one's best projects are completed in the last two years of school, with the finest projects completed in the last studio courses. There is merit in presenting the most recent projects first and working backward.

Grouping projects in terms of scope and function also has merit because it allows one to target certain areas for certain interviews. For example, if hospitality projects are clustered together, one can focus on them in an interview with a hospitality-oriented firm. When clustering projects functionally, it is common to lead with the strongest projects and work backward.

Organizing projects purely in terms of quality also has merit. Presenting the strongest projects first can generate excitement. This allows for weaker projects to be seen as building blocks. I think it is a mistake to lead with weak projects in the hope that you will build excitement as quality increases. Weak projects, seen too early, will generally put off a potential employer. Moreover, there is always the possibility that the potential employer will be called away in the middle of the interview, not having seen the best work.

One of the biggest problems for interior designers in creating entry-level portfolios is the size and weight of many presentation boards. It is difficult to include many thick boards of mounted materials in a standard zipper portfolio case with plastic sleeves. One way around this problem is to include all drawings, renderings, and graphics simply

Figure 8-14a
Student project booklet
(exterior) created for a furniture
design class.
By Sarah Amundsen.
Photograph by Bill Wikrent.

Figure 8-14b
Student project booklet opened
to display sketches and finished
product.
By Sarah Amundsen.
Photograph by Bill Wikrent.

mounted on paper or copied onto paper, held inside sleeves. Only materials presentations are then mounted on paperboard. The materials boards can be removed from the portfolio and presented as the employer reviews the project drawings in the sleeves.

Some recent graduates opt for a thin box-like portfolio and present all projects mounted on boards or plates. The boards are carried to the interview in the portfolio or presentation case, then removed and handed in stacks to the interviewer. Some students decide that they wish to have a more compact portfolio and choose to reduce all project documents to fit a smaller case. This creates a manageable portfolio; however, reducing all student work is time-consuming and expensive.

8-15a

Figure 8-15a
Student project booklet
(exterior) created for an interior
design studio project.
By Ardella Pieper.
Photograph by Bill Wikrent.

Practicing designers usually have photographs taken of built projects and combine these with sketches and reduced working drawings. Photographs, sketches, and reduced drawings can be included in small, very manageable portfolios or binders. Figure 8-13 illustrates some popular portfolios and presentation cases.

Some design graduates manage the size problem by presenting multiple portfolio cases. This is most often done with special projects, such as a thesis or long term project. Putting special projects into separate portfolios can add interest to the presentation. However, it may be a mistake to use more than two individual portfolios because they can become difficult to handle if the applicant is nervous. Figures 8-14a, 8-14b, 8-15a, and 8-15b are samples of project notebooks.

In the case of technical drawings, it is perfectly appropriate to hand them to an interviewer as flat, stapled sheets, rolled drawings, or compiled into a small booklet. These drawings, such as construction documents and CADD drawings, are important to bring to interviews and are often presented outside the traditional portfolio case. It is worth practicing arriving in the room for the interview with a portfolio case and rolls of drawings. Remember, you will need to shake someone's hand at the same time you are setting down your portfolio, drawings, and perhaps a coat or bag.

It is important to include design process documents with finished presentation drawings in the portfolio. Employers often wish to see how a potential employee thinks and the nature of his or her design process. The best way to document the design process in student projects is to save everything—all research, notes, doodles, schedules, bubble diagrams, sketches, and so forth. At the end of the project these process documents and sketches can be photocopied and bound into a project booklet. The project booklet is then available for discussion during the interview. Retaining sketches, notes, and drawings is also important for practicing designers, who should keep these items for reference (and for interviews).

Figure 8-15b
Student project booklet
(in use) created for an interior
design studio project.
By Ardella Pieper.
Photograph by Bill Wikrent.

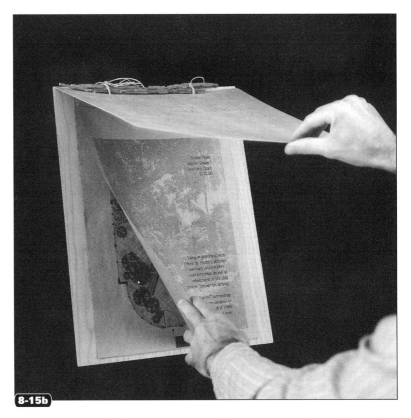

8-15b

REFERENCES

Berryman, Gregg. *Designing Creative Portfolios.*
Menlo Park, CA: Crisp Publications, 1994.

Berryman, Gregg. *Designing Creative Resumes.*
Menlo Park, CA: Crisp Publications, 1990.

Bostwick, Burdette. Bostwick. *Resume Writing.*
New York: John Wiley & Sons, 1990.

Fry, Ron. *Your First Resume.* Hawthorne, NJ:
Career Press, 1992.

Jute, André. *Grids: The Structure of Graphic Design.*
New York: Watson-Guptill Publications, 1996.

Linton, Harold. *Portfolio Design.* New York:
W.W. Norton, 1996.

Marquand, Ed. *Graphic Design Presentations.*
New York: Van Nostrand Reinhold, 1986.

Oldach, Mark. *Creativity for Graphic Designers.*
Cincinnati, OH: North Light Books, 1995.

Swan, Alan. *The New Graphic Design School.*
New York: John Wiley & Sons, 1997.

Williams, Robin. *The Little Mac Book.* Berkeley,
CA: Peachpit Press, 1995.

Clearly, developing a successful resume and portfolio takes work, talent, and time. The graphic design and organization of these elements deserves careful consideration and a serious look inward. By taking an honest inventory of your objectives, work, interests, talents, and skills, you can design a system that communicates your identity to potential employers. Developing a schedule and budget for your portfolio system in your final semester in school is extremely helpful. Researching potential employers and firms early in your last year of school is highly advisable. Practicing professionals are well advised to save everything (make copies!) for inclusion in a future portfolio, because in a designer's life learning never ends.

Directory of Professionals Featured

Craig Beddow, AIA
Beddow Design · Digital Architecture
4036 Colfax Avenue South
Minneapolis, MN 55409

Bruck Allen Architects Inc.
11452 El Camino Real, Ste. 200
San Diego, CA 92130

CNH Architects Inc.
7300 West 147th Street, Ste. 504
St. Paul, MN 55124

Aj Dumas
Mind's Eye Design
2681 118th Street
Chippewa Falls, WI 54729

Ellerbe Becket
800 LaSalle Avenue
Minneapolis, MN 55402-2014

Bob Feyereisen
Feyereisen Studios
2101 Kennedy Street, N.E., Studio 201
Minneapolis, MN 55413

Kathy Fogerty
1070 Ashland
St. Paul, MN 55104

Janet Lawson
Architectural Illustration
112 North Third Street, Suite 206
Minneapolis, MN 55401

Peter Lee
1331 North East Tyler, Studio 232
Minneapolis, MN 55413

Meyer, Scherer & Rockcastle Ltd.
119 North Second Street
Minneapolis, MN 55401-1420

Courtney Nystuen
Tech Wing
University of Wisconsin-Stout
Menomonie, WI 54751

Thomas Oliphant Studio
1500 Jackson Street, N.E.
Minneapolis, MN 55413

Jeff Rabkin
2101 Kennedy Street, N.E., Studio 204
Minneapolis, MN 55413

Arthur Shuster Inc.
1995 Oakcrest Avenue West
St. Paul, MN 55113

Smart Associates
119 North Fourth Street, Ste. 506
Minneapolis, MN 55401

Bill Wikrent
Learning Technology Services-Photography/
Multi-Media
University of Wisconsin-Stout
Menomonie, WI 54751

Appendix *2*

Color Theory for Rendering

Color rendering requires a basic understanding of color theory. One key aspect of color rendering is understanding the properties of color and how to approximate these properties with various media or pigments.

Hue. What we often call a color should actually be referred to as a hue. Green and orange are both hues. Hue is changed only when mixed with another hue. Green mixed with blue changes the hue to greenish blue.

Value. The term value refers to lightness or darkness. Adding white lightens a color without changing the hue; this is also true of adding black to darken a color.

Chroma. Also referred to as intensity or saturation, chroma describes the purity or level of brightness of a color. Describing something as being dull or bright is a way of referring to chroma.

Hue, value, and chroma are all properties of color and are part of color rendering. Consider the following example. When rendering a faded red chair, we must select the correct hue—red. The red must not be bright, but faded; this means the chroma is not highly saturated. The chair must have light, medium, and dark values applied to various locations based on the light source—these values are necessary in rendering.

When using markers, the following can be done to achieve properties of color:

Hue. The perfect marker hue is sometimes available; however, in many cases a desired hue of marker does not exist. Layering two marker hues can sometimes produce the appropriate hue. For example, red-orange is often created by layering orange and red. In some cases the hue can be altered with the application of colored pencil over the marker color. Hue is also altered by making a pool of color on tracing paper and "picking it up" with a colorless blender; the blender is then dabbed on in the desired locations.

Value. The best way to create value with markers is to lay gray marker in the appropriate locations prior to the colored marker application. This is done by locating the light, medium, and dark areas of the form, then, light, medium and gray markers can be underlaid. Colored marker is then applied on top of the gray, and the values are complete. Sometimes the complementary color may be underlaid in place of gray. A wash of gray or complementary colored pencil may also be applied on top of marker in the appropriate locations.

To create highlights or light areas, it is sometimes necessary to wash over marker with light-colored pencil, especially white or beige. Washes of dry pastel may also be used to lighten or darken areas and to achieve value gradation. Small amounts of white gouache or white-out pen (pen only—not liquid from a bottle) also work for highlights.

Chroma. Marker chroma is often dulled by the application of a layer of complementary-hued marker, colored pencil, or dry pastel. Chroma may be brightened with the application of a similar hue of marker, pencil, or pastel. For example, to brighten dull green marker color, apply a brighter green colored pencil layer on top of the marker.

It is worthwhile to experiment with multiple layers of markers, washes of pencil, and pastel to vary hue, chroma, and value to enrich a rendering.

3

Scale Figures and Entourage

Adding scale figures to orthographic projections, perspectives, and paraline drawings provides a touch of realism and clarifies relative proportions. Adding plants, animals, and other elements of everyday life can also enliven drawings.

A number of books are available with scaled figures and entourage elements such as plants, cars, boats, and sports equipment. These books contain hundreds of images, free of copyright restrictions, that are easily traced onto transparent paper. Images from magazines can also be traced into drawings. Many designers prefer to draw their own scale figures, reflective of personal style. Figure A-1 shows a step-by-step creation of stylized human figures.

Human figures must be placed at the appropriate height and locations in a drawing. In orthographic projections and paraline drawings adult figures should be drawn with eye levels at about 5 to 6 feet. In perspective drawings, adult

figures should be placed with eye level at about 5 to 6 feet, which is the standard horizon line location. In perspectives drawn with nonstandard horizon lines (those above or below eye level) scale figures are placed at 5 to 6 feet, which may be far above or below the horizon line. Figure A-2 shows placement of human figures in two-point perspective.

I recommend keeping a file filled with entourage elements such as plants, window coverings, and decorative objects. Mail order catalogs, plant catalogs, equipment catalogs, and magazines provide excellent images for entourage elements. Items from a clip file can be drawn or traced, using a quick stylized approach that allows for elimination of details. These traced items should be simplified to speed the drawing process and to avoid overwhelming the drawing compositionally. Figure A-3 shows examples of plants drawn in a quick, stylized manner.

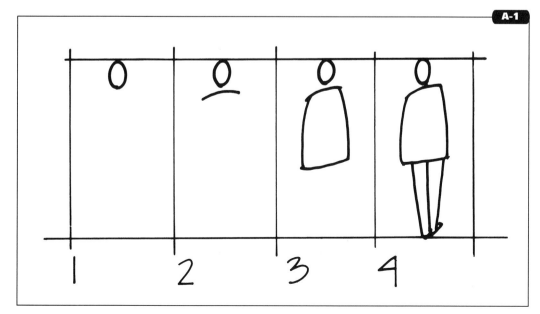

A-1

Figure A-1
Step-by-step drawing of
human figures.
1. Draw a small oval head.
2. Draw curved shoulders s
lightly below head.
3. Draw torso extending
downward from shoulders.
4. Draw legs below torso;
legs can be slightly uneven.

Figure A-3
Plants and other entourage
elements can be simplified
for inclusion in presentation
drawings.

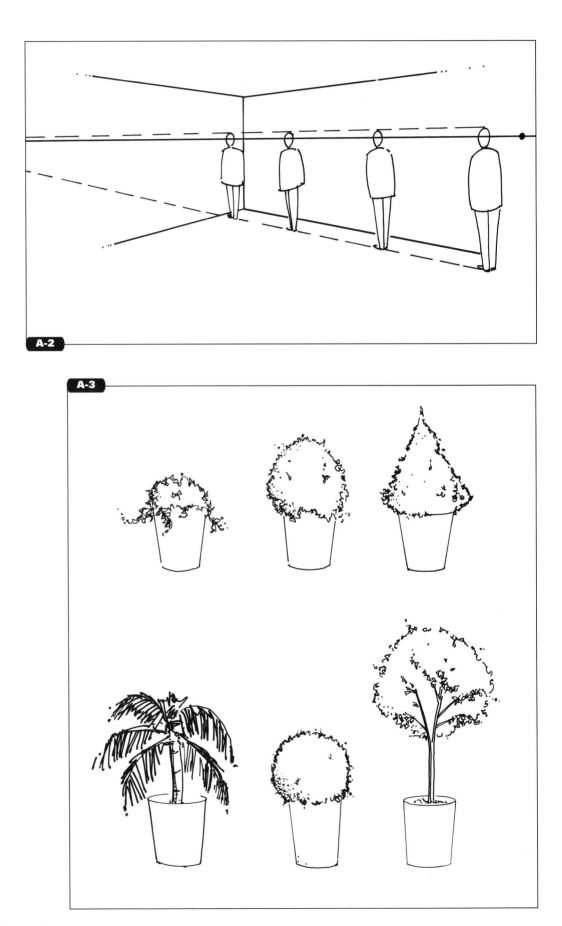

A-2

A-3

Appendix 4

Floor Plans of Professional Case Study, Science Museum of Minnesota

Figure A-4
Floor plan, level five, Science
Museum of Minnesota.
By Ellerbe Becket.
Courtesy of Ellerbe Becket
and the Science Museum
of Minnesota.

Appendix | **173**

Figure A-5
Floor plan, level six, Science Museum of Minnesota.
By Ellerbe Becket.
Courtesy of Ellerbe Becket and the Science Museum of Minnesota.

Index

Adhesive reproduction film, described, 4

Adhesives, scale models, 113, 115, 118–120

Airbrush, rendering, 89

American Institute of Architects (AIA), design process, 22

Analysis, design process, 22

Appliqué film. *See* Adhesive reproduction film

Architectural scale, described, 6

Art markers, rendering, 87–88

Art papers, rendering, 85

Balsa foam, scale models, 114–115

Balsa wood, scale models, 113

Basswood, scale models, 113

Blocking diagrams, schematic design, 31–33

Blueprinting. *See* Diazo reproduction

Bond paper, rendering, 83

Bristol paper, rendering, 85

Bubble diagrams, schematic design, 29–30

Ceiling plans. *See* Reflected ceiling plans

Chipboard, scale models, 112

Collage, rendering, 90

Color, rendering, 94–96

Colored paper, rendering, 84–85

Colored pencils, rendering, 86–87

Color movement, rendering, 106

Color variation, rendering, 106

Compass, described, 7

Computer aided drafting and design (CADD):
  blocking diagrams, 33
  lettering, 16–17
  orthographic drawing, 19–21
  perspective drawing, 76–80
  portfolio design, 164, 167
  technology and, 1

Conceptual design, schematic design, 35–36

Cone of vision, perspective drawing, 51

Construction documents:
  defined, 7
  design process, 22

Contract administration, design process, 22

Corrugated board, scale models, 112

Cover letters, writing of, 160–162

Design development:
  described, 40–42
  design process, 22

Design process, 22–42
  design development phase, 40–42
  overview, 22
  programming, 23–27
  schematic design, 28–40. *See also* Schematic design

Diagonal lines, perspective drawing, 53

Diazo reproduction:
  described, 2
  rendering, 85

Dimensions, orthographic drawing, 18–19

Diminution of size, perspective drawing, 51

Disposable technical pens, described, 5

Doors, floor plans, 10

Double-sided tape, scale models, 119

Drafting, defined, 1

Drafting tape, described, 6

Drafting vellum:
  described, 3
  rendering, 83

Drawing. *See* Orthographic drawing; Perspective drawing

Drawing board, described, 6

Drawing pencils, described, 4–5

Drawing surfaces:
  described, 2–4
  rendering, 83–86

Dry cleaning pads, described, 5
Dry pastels, rendering, 88–89

Electric eraser, described, 6
    Elevations. *See* Interior elevations
Ellipses, perspective drawing, 56–60
Erasers, described, 5–6
Eraser shield, described, 5
Estimated one-point perspective, drawing of, 61–63
Estimated two-point perspective, drawing of, 63–67
Evaluation, design process, 22

Felt-tip pens, described, 5–6
Fit plans, stacking plans and, schematic design, 33–35
Flexible curve, described, 7
Flip-up models, construction of, 122–124
Floor plans:
    described, 9–13
    interior elevations and, 13
Foam, scale models, 113–115
Foam board, scale models, III
French curve, described, 7
Furniture, scale models, 126

Gator Board, scale models, III–II2
Gouache, rendering, 89
Graphite:
    described, 4
    rendering, 83, 86
Grid charts. *See* Prepared perspective grid charts
Grids, portfolios and resumes, 147–149
Guidelines, lettering, 17

Hand-made paper, rendering, 85
Horizon line, perspective drawing, 49
Horizontal building section. *See* Floor plans
Hot glue, scale models, 120

Ideation sketches, defined, 7
Illumination, rendering, 81–82
Illustration board:
    rendering, 85
    scale models, II2
Ink, rendering, 86
Instant glues, scale models, II9
Interior design:
    defined, xii
    practice of, xi–xii
    technology and, I
Interior elevations, described, 9, 13–14

Isometric drawings, paraline drawing, 47-48
Keys, materials presentations, 138-141
Knives, scale models, 120
Kraft paper, rendering, 85

Lead holders, described, 5
Lead pointer, described, 5
Legends, materials presentations, 138–141
Lettering, described, 16–18
Line-making implements, described, 4–7
Line weight:
    floor plans, 9–10
    interior elevations, 13

Major axis, perspective drawing, 56–57
Marker paper, rendering, 83
Markers, rendering, 87–88
Mark-making implements, described, 4–7
Masking tape, scale models, II9
Material qualities, rendering, 92-94
Materials presentations, 131-146
    materials and media, 133-135
    organization and composition, 135-138
    overview, 131-133
        techniques, 141-146
        total presentation, 145-146
    window matting, 143, 145
    titles, keys, and legends, 138-141
Matrices, programming, described, 26-27
Mechanical pencils, described, 5
Minor axis, perspective drawing, 57
Mounting boards, rendering, 85

North arrow, floor plans, 12

One-point perspective:
    estimated, drawing of, 61-63
    perspective drawing, 51
Orthographic drawing, 1-21
    computer aided drafting and design (CADD), 19-21
    dimensions, 18-19
    drawing surfaces, 2-4
    floor plans, 9-13
    interior elevations, 13-14
    lettering, 16-18
    line- and mark-making implements, 4-7
    reflected ceiling plans, 15-16
    rendering of, 90-96
    sections, 15
    three-dimensional drawing compared, 43
    types of, 7-9

Orthographic projection, defined, 7

Painters tape, scale models, 119

Paper, rendering, 83–86

Paperboards, scale models, 110–113

Paraline drawing, 44–48

   isometric drawings, 47–48

   overview, 43

   plan oblique drawings, 44–47

   tools for, 44

Parallel rulers, described, 6

Pattern, rendering, 92–94

Pencils:

   described, 4–5

   rendering, 83, 86–87

Pens, rendering, 86

Perspective drawing, 48–60, 61–80

   basics of, 49–51

   computer aided drafting and design (CADD),
      76–80

   estimated one-point perspective, 61–63

   estimated two-point perspective, 63–67

   importance of, 48–49

   one-point perspective, 51

   overview, 43

   photograph tracing, 73–76

   prepared grid charts, 72–73

   refined linear drawing, 67–68

   rendering, 97–108

   three-point perspective, 52

   tools for, 44

   two-point perspective, 52

   two-point plan projection method, 68–71

   visual skills development, 52–60

Photograph tracing, perspective drawing, 73–76

Picture plane:

   defined, 7

   perspective drawing, 49

Plan, defined, 9

Plan oblique drawings, paraline drawing, 44–47

Plastic drafting film, described, 3–4

Plastics, scale models, 113–115

Portfolios and resumes, 147–168

   cover letters, 160–162

   graphic design components, 147–150

      grids, 147–149

      typefaces, 149–150

   overview, 147

   portfolio design, 162–168

   resumes, 150–160

      samples of, 153–159

      writing of, 150–152, 160

Precut drafting dots, described, 6

Prepared perspective grid charts, use of, 72–73

Presentation drawings:

   defined, 7

   schematic design, 37–40

Presentation materials. *See* Materials presentations

Print paper, rendering, 85

Programming, 23–27

   design process, 22

   overview, 23–25

   programming analysis graphics, 25–26

   programming matrices, 26–27

Programming analysis graphics, described, 25–26

Programming matrices, described, 26–27

Refined linear drawing, perspective drawing, 67–68

Reflected ceiling plans, described, 15–16

Rendering, 81–108

   illumination, 81–82

   importance of, 81

   media, 86–90

   orthographic projection drawings, 90–96

   paper and drawing surfaces, 83–86

   perspective drawings, 97–108

Resumes. *See* Portfolios and resumes

Rubber cement, scale models, 119

Scale, floor plans, 9

Scale models, 109–130

   construction, 120–130

      flip-up models, 122–124

      practical applications, 124–130

      study models, 120–121

   materials and tools, 110–120

      adhesives, 115, 118–120

      paperboards, 110–112

      plastics and foam, 113v115

      wood, 113

   types of, 109–110

Scale notation, floor plans, 12

Schematic design, 28–40

   blocking diagrams, 31–33

   bubble diagrams, 29–30

   conceptual design, 35–36

   design process, 22

   fit plans and stacking plans, 33–35

   overview, 28–29

   presentation graphics, 37–40

Sections:
    defined, 9
Sections:
    described, 15
Solvents, rendering, 87
Spray adhesive, scale models, 119–120
Stacking plans, fit plans and, schematic design, 33–35
Stairs:
    floor plans, 10
    vanishing trace, 53, 56
Station point, perspective drawing, 49, 51
Studio markers, rendering, 87–88
Styrene, scale models, 114
Symbols, floor plans, 12
Synthesis, design process, 22

Technical pens, described, 5
Technology. *See also* Computer aided drafting and
        design (CADD)
    interior design and, 1
    lettering, 16–17
Templates:
    described, 6–7
    ellipses, 58
Texture, rendering, 92–94
Three-dimensional drawing, orthographic drawing
        compared, 43. *See also* Perspective drawing
Three-point perspective, perspective drawing, 52
Titles:
    floor plans, 12
    materials presentations, 138-141
Tracing, of photographs, perspective drawing, 73–76
Tracing paper:
    described, 2–3
    rendering, 83
Transfer paper, rendering, 84
Transfer tape, scale models, 119
Triangles, described, 6
T squares, described, 6
Two-point perspective:
    estimated, drawing of, 63–67
    perspective drawing, 52
Two-point plan projection method, described, 68–71
Typefaces, portfolios and resumes, 149–150

Vanishing point, perspective drawing, 49, 53
Vanishing trace, perspective drawing, 53, 56
Vellum. *See* Drafting vellum
Vertical measuring line, perspective drawing, 53
Visualizing paper, rendering, 83

Visual skills development, perspective drawing, 52–60

Watercolor paper, rendering, 85–86
Watercolors, rendering, 89
White glue, scale models, 113, 115
Window matting, materials presentations, 143, 145
Windows, floor plans, 10
Wood, scale models, 113
Wooden drawing pencils. *See* Pencils
Working drawings. *See* Construction documents

X-acto knives, scale models, 120